ALL LOVER THE PLACE

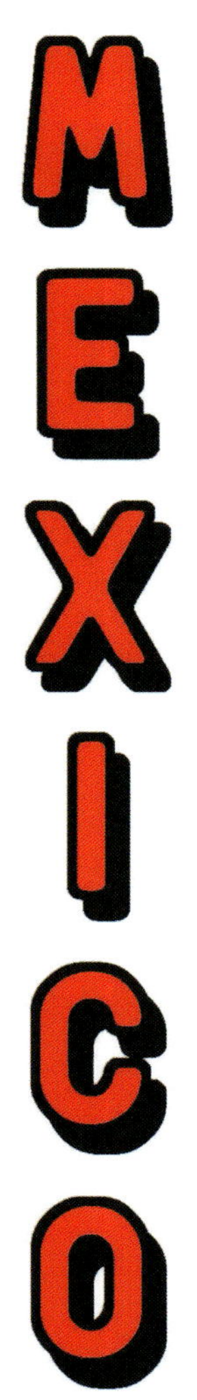
MEXICO

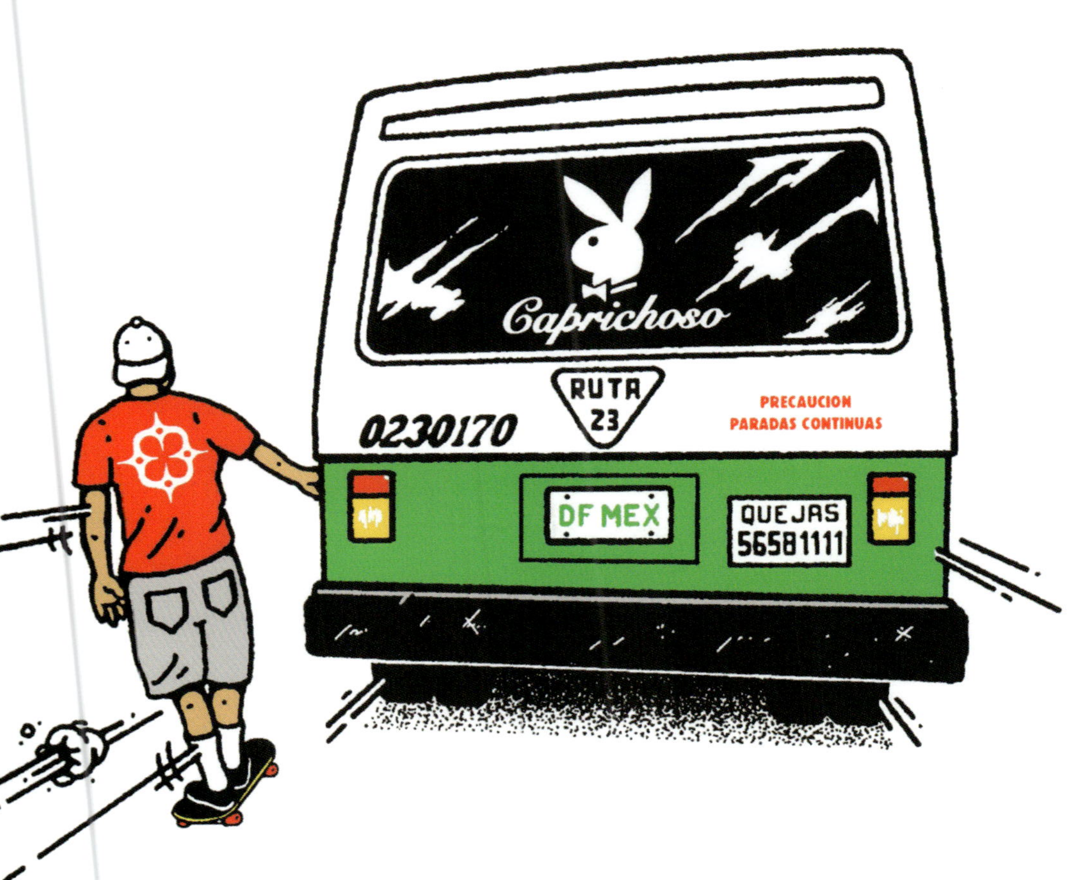
Caprichoso
RUTA
23
0230170
PRECAUCION
PARADAS CONTINUAS
DF MEX
QUEJAS
56581111

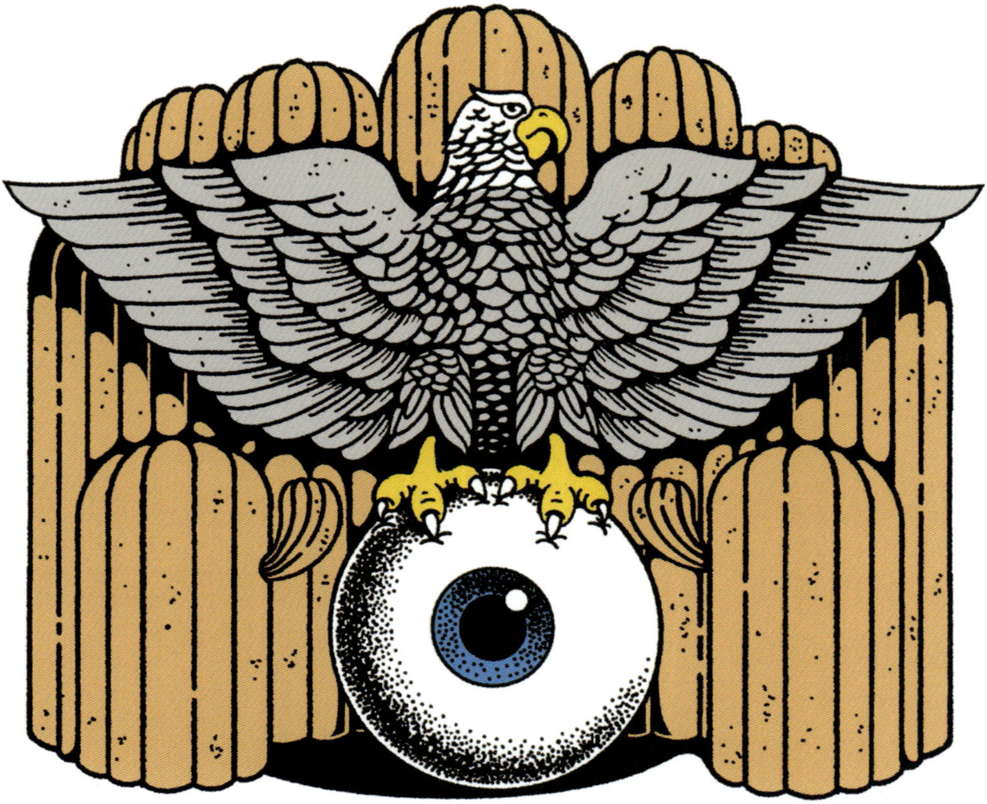

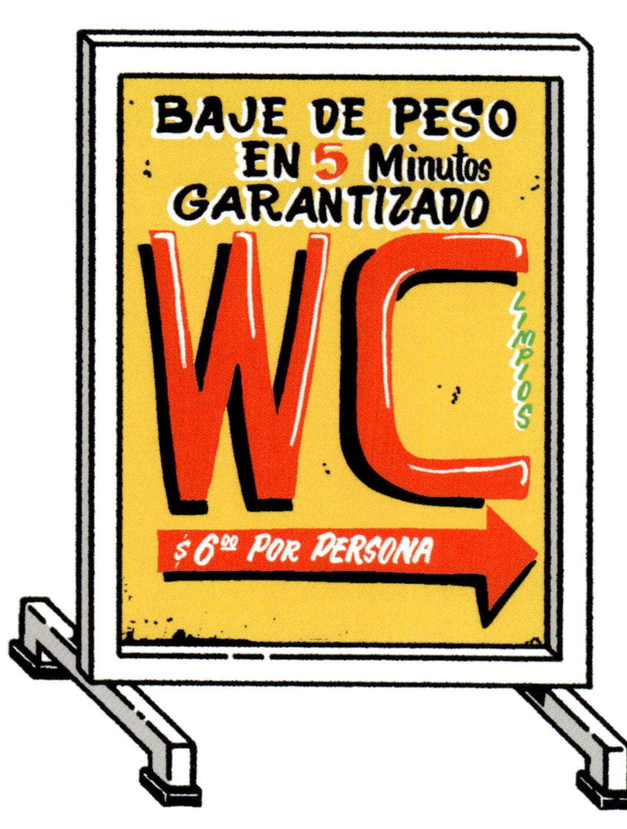
BAJE DE PESO
EN 5 Minutos
GARANTIZADO
WC
LIMPIOS
$6.00 POR PERSONA

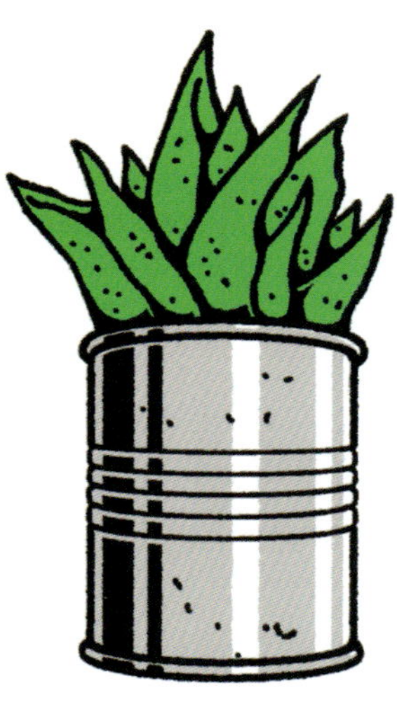

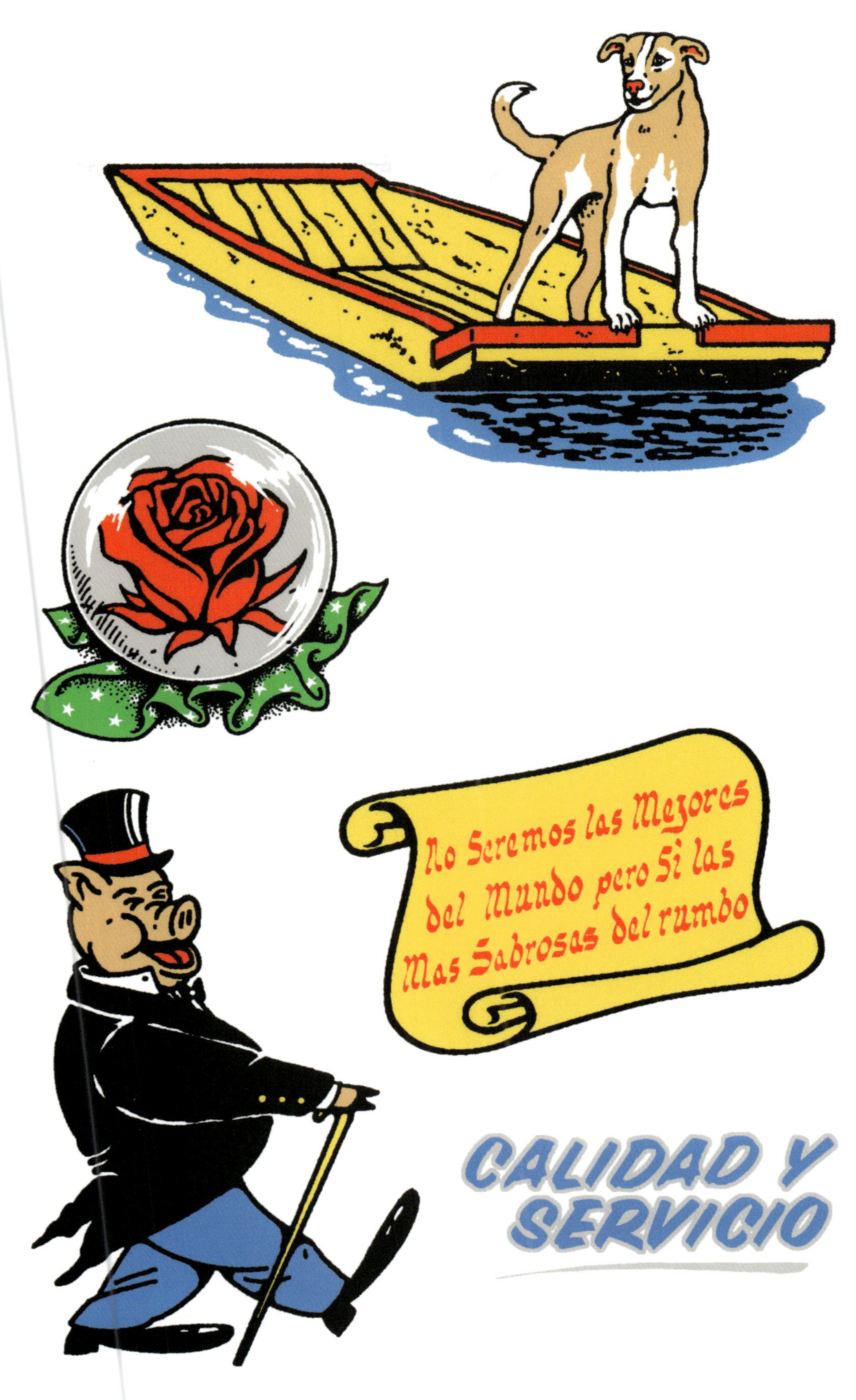
No Seremos las Mejores
del Mundo pero Si las
Mas Sabrosas del rumbo
CALIDAD Y
SERVICIO

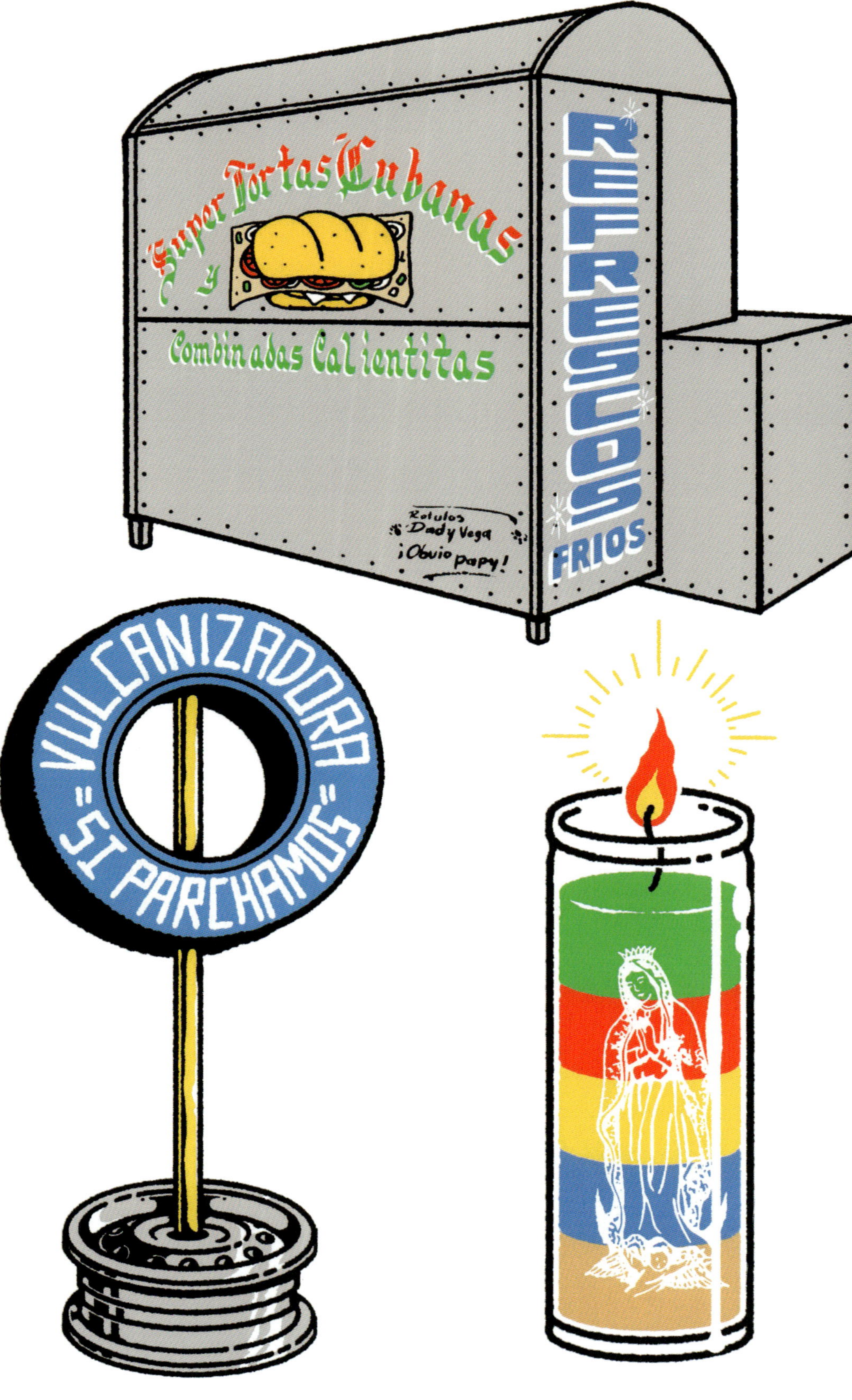
Super Tortas Cubanas
y
Combinadas Calientitas
REFRESCOS
FRIOS
Rotulos
Dady Vega
¡Obvio papy!
VULCANIZADORA
"SI PARCHAMOS"

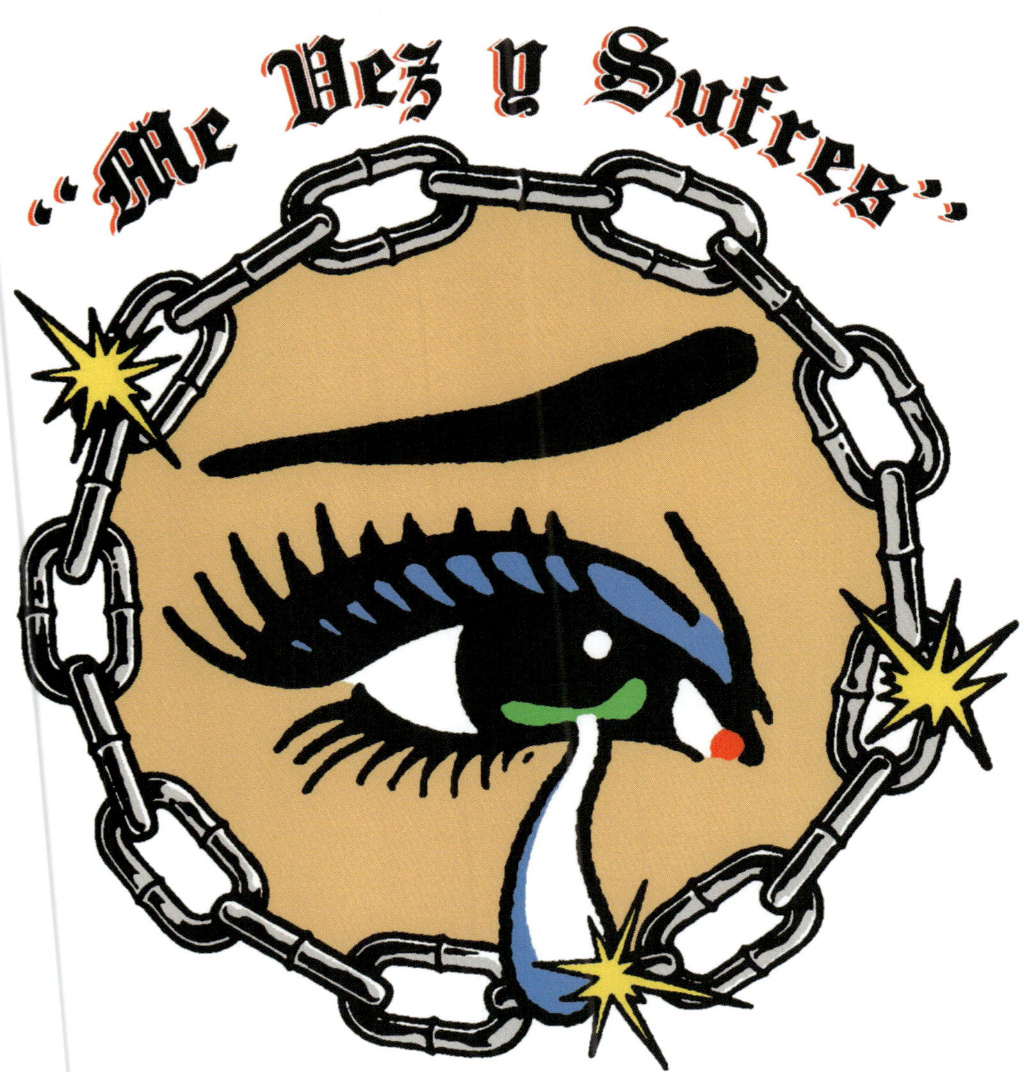
"Me Vez y Sufres"

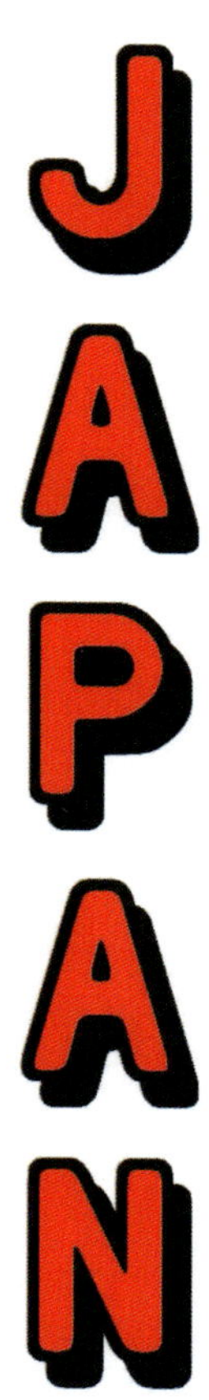
JAPAN

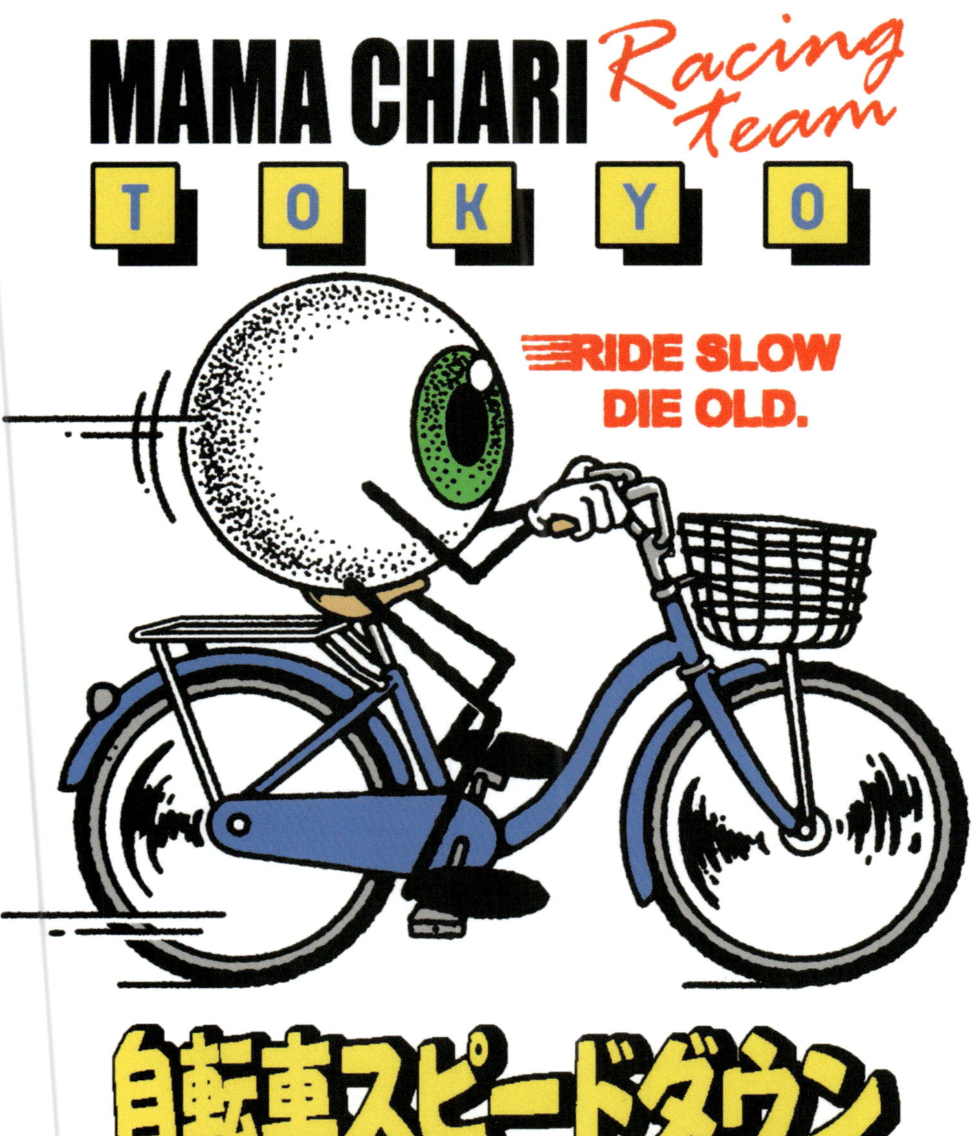
MAMA CHARI
Racing team
TOKYO
RIDE SLOW
DIE OLD.
自転車スピードダウン

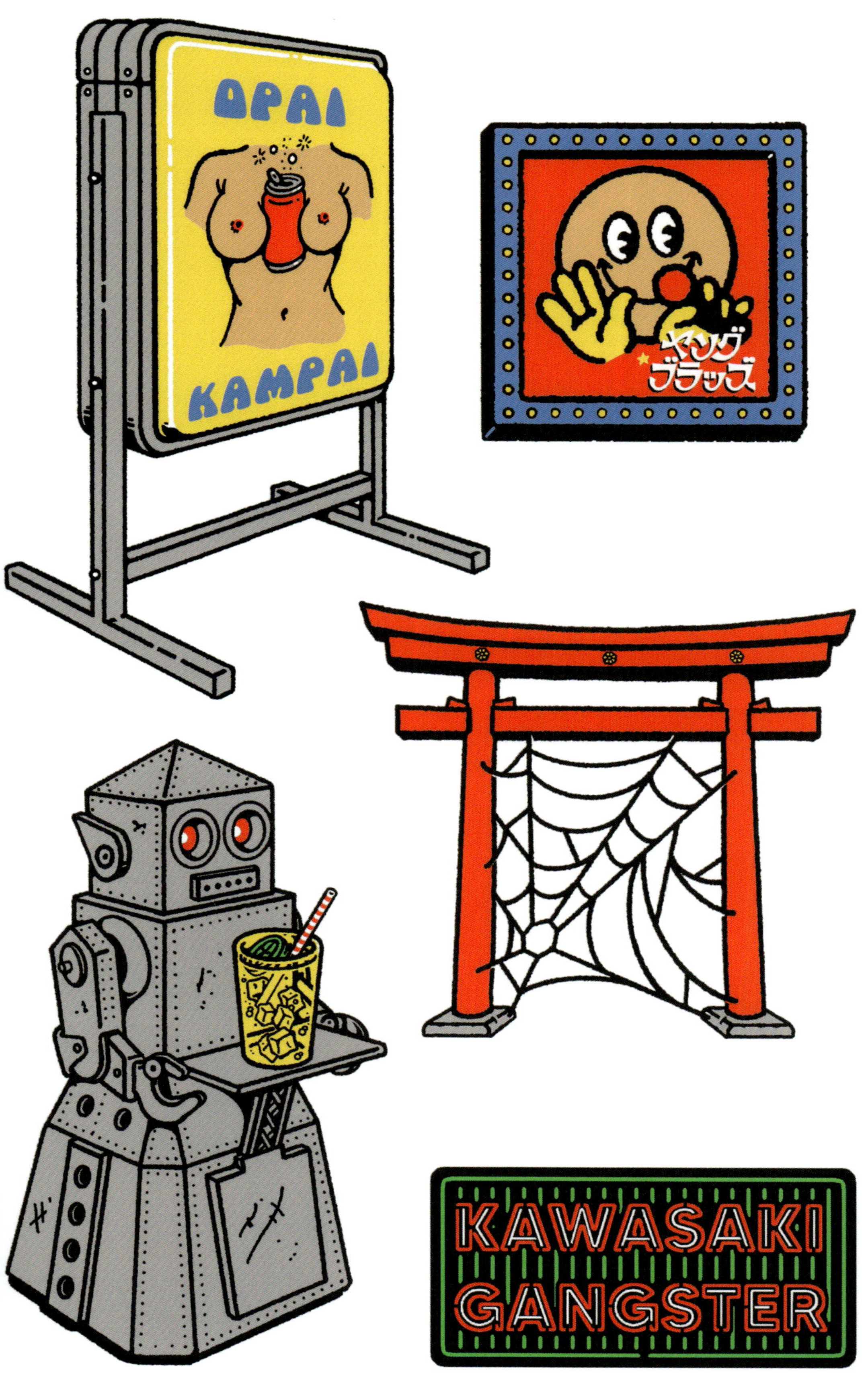
OPAI
KAMPAI
ヤング
ブラッズ
KAWASAKI
GANGSTER

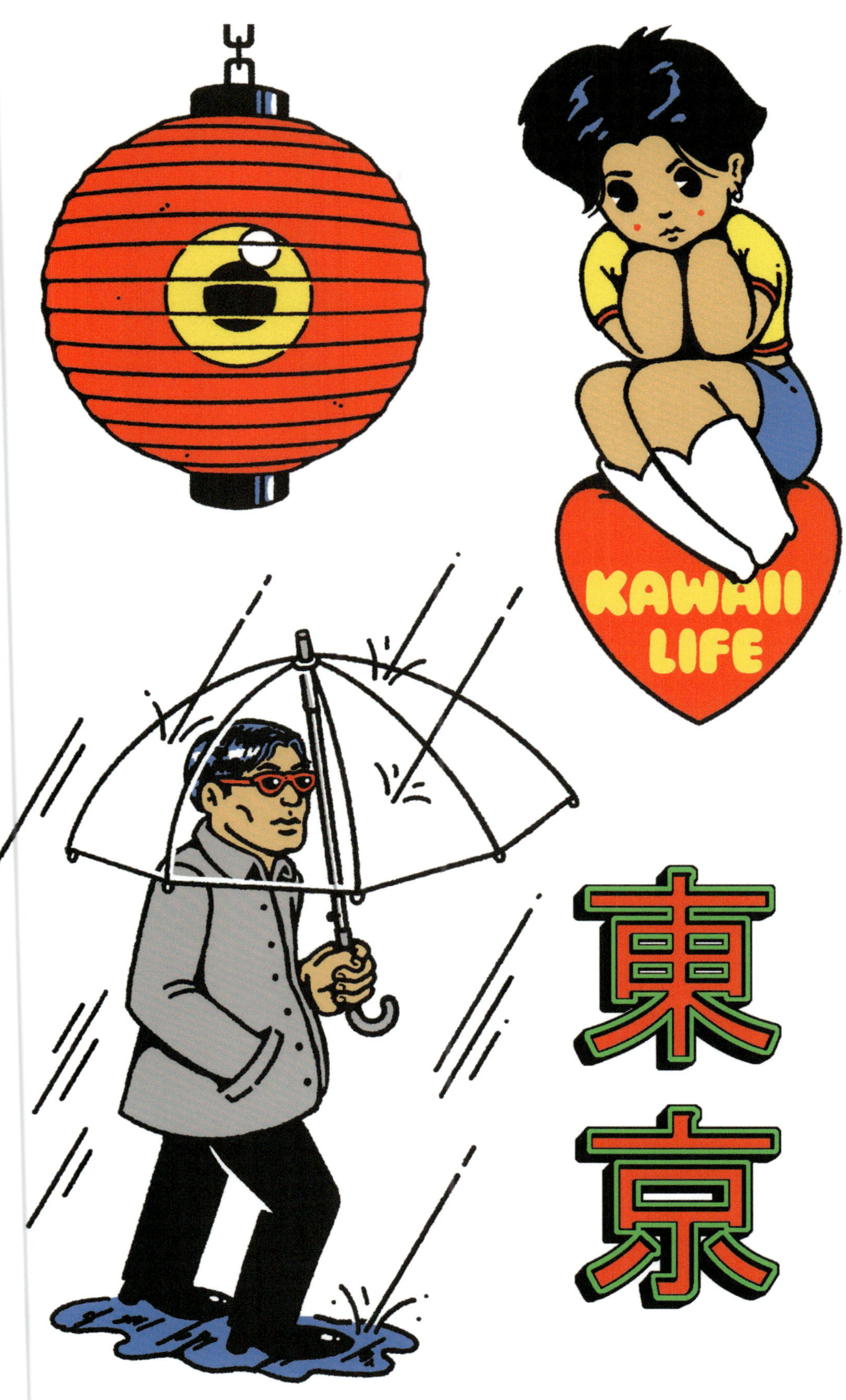
KAWAII
LIFE
東
京

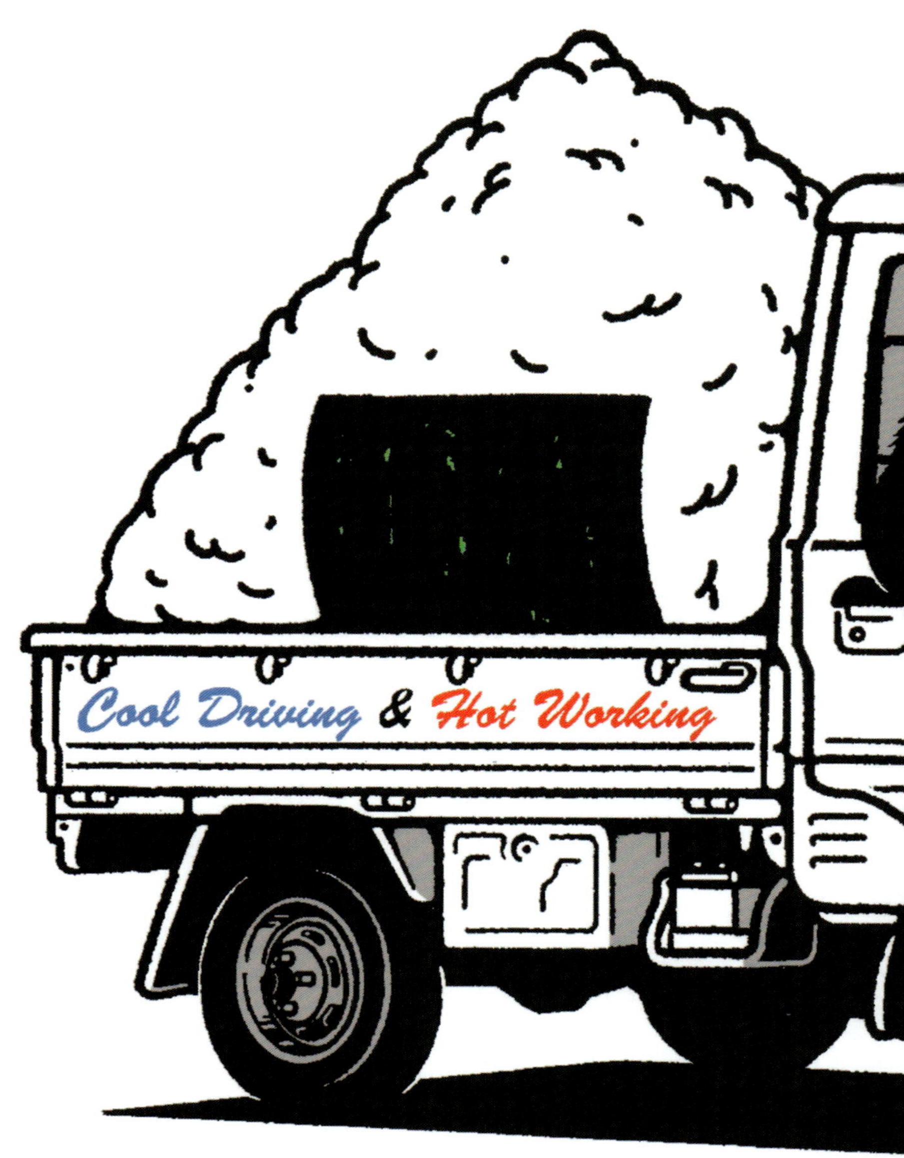
Cool Driving & Hot Working

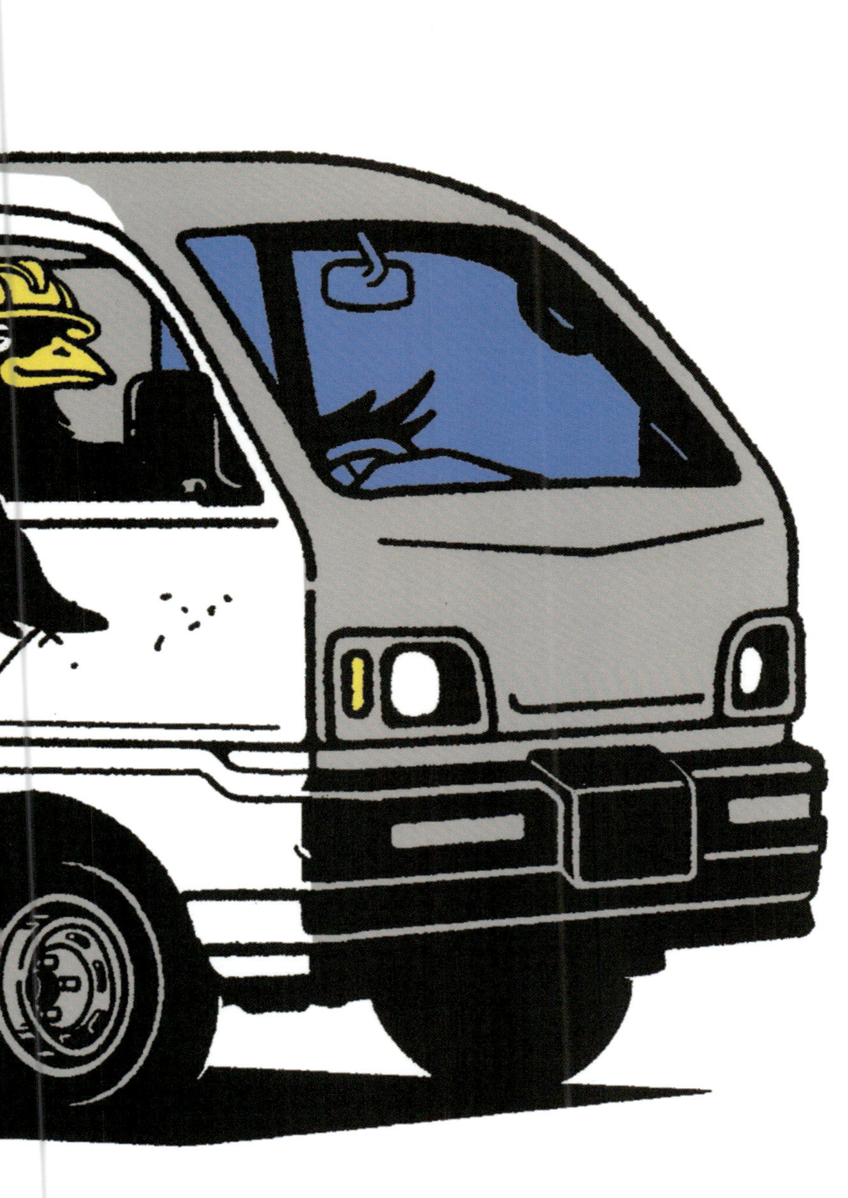

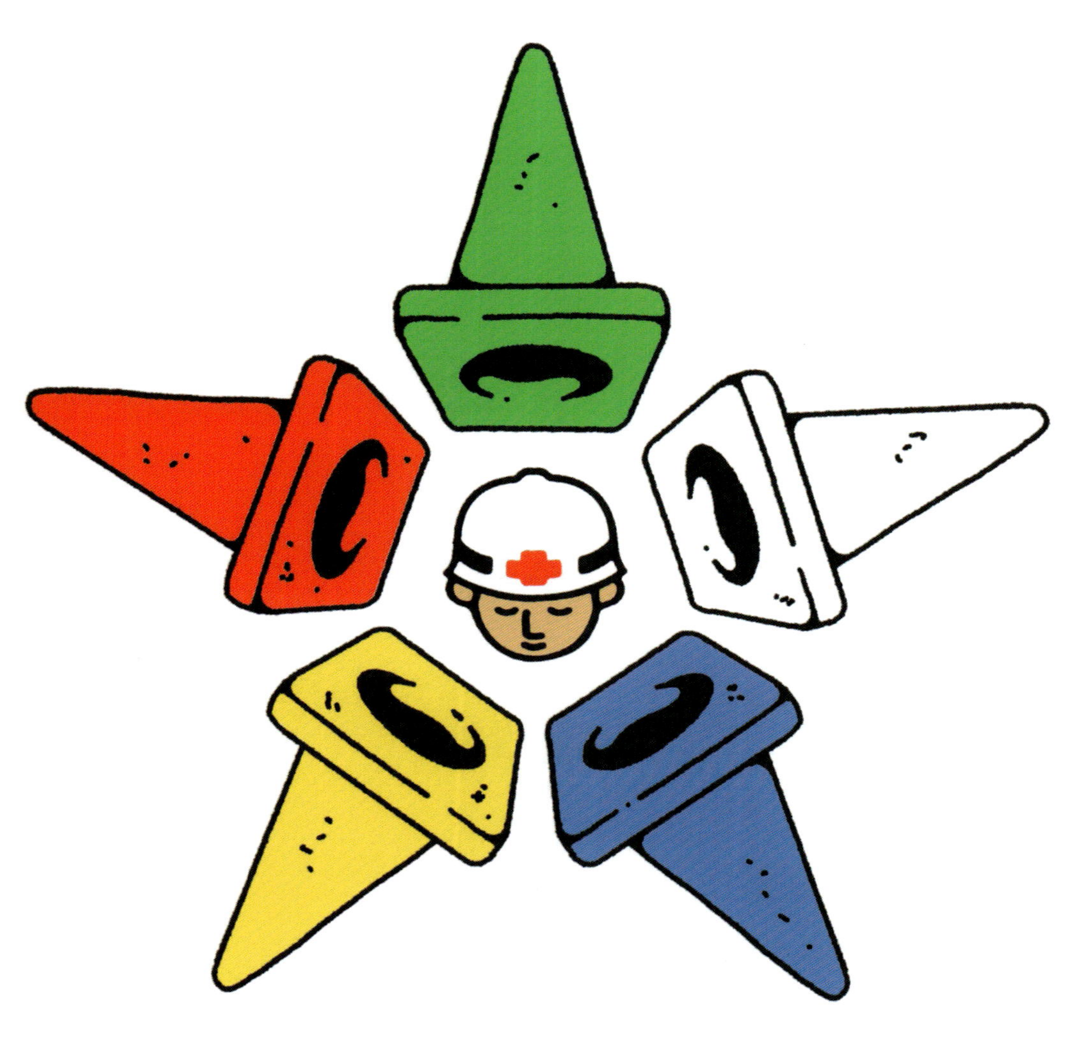

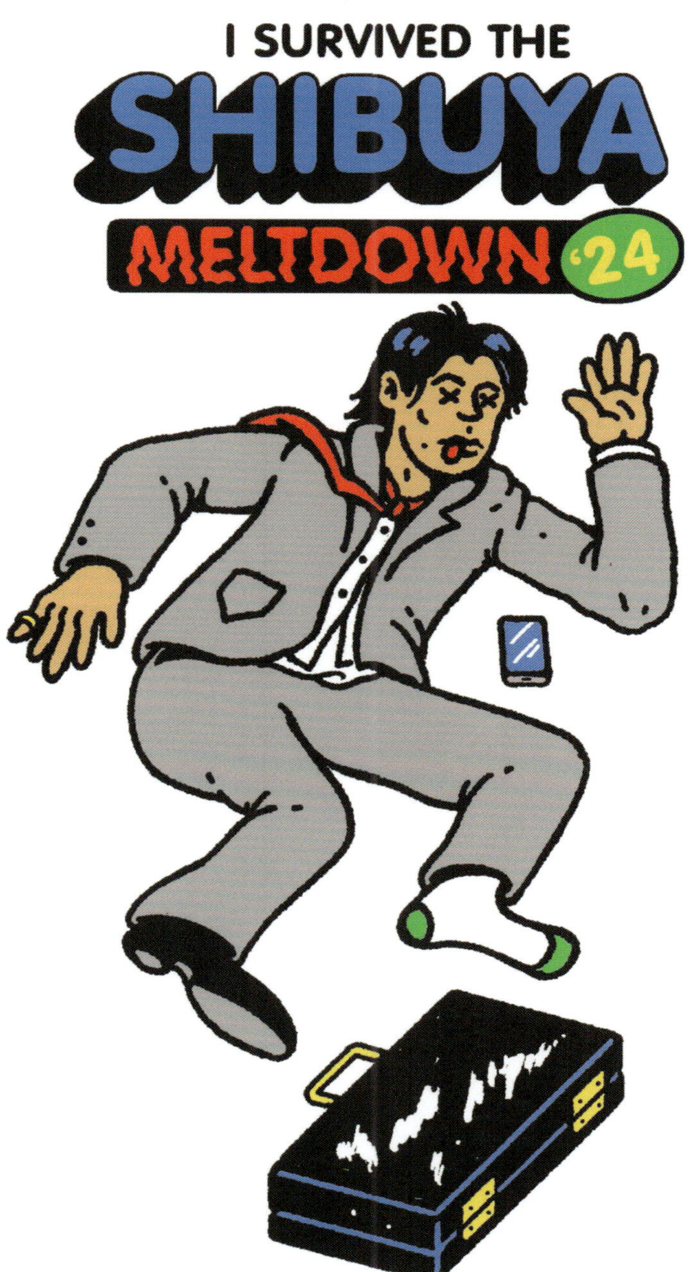
I SURVIVED THE
SHIBUYA
MELTDOWN '24

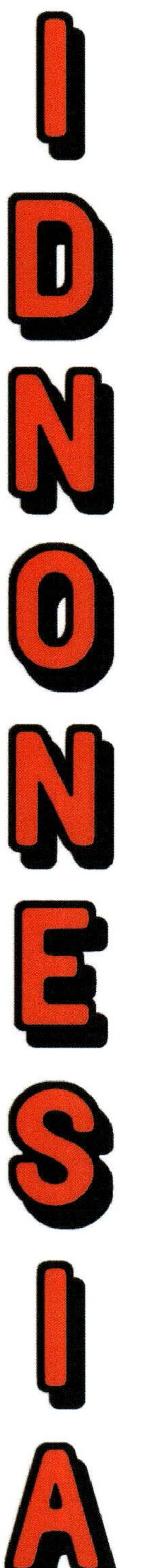
IDNONESIA

BULE HUNTER

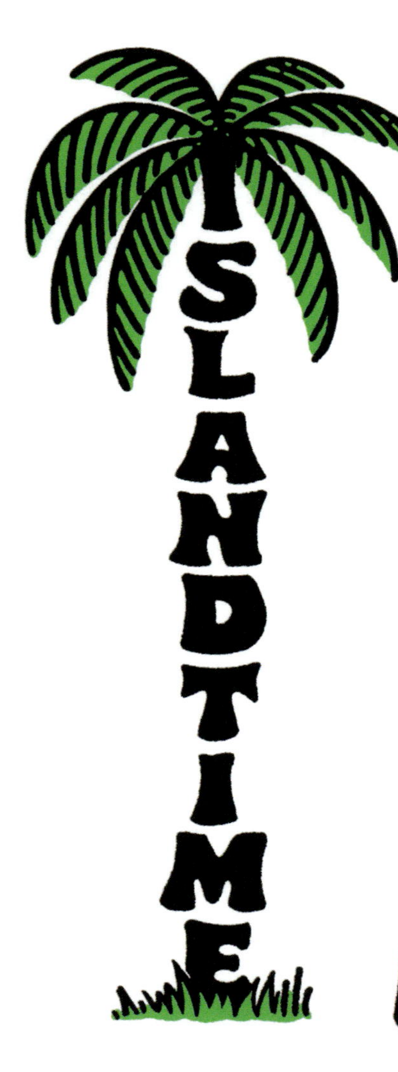

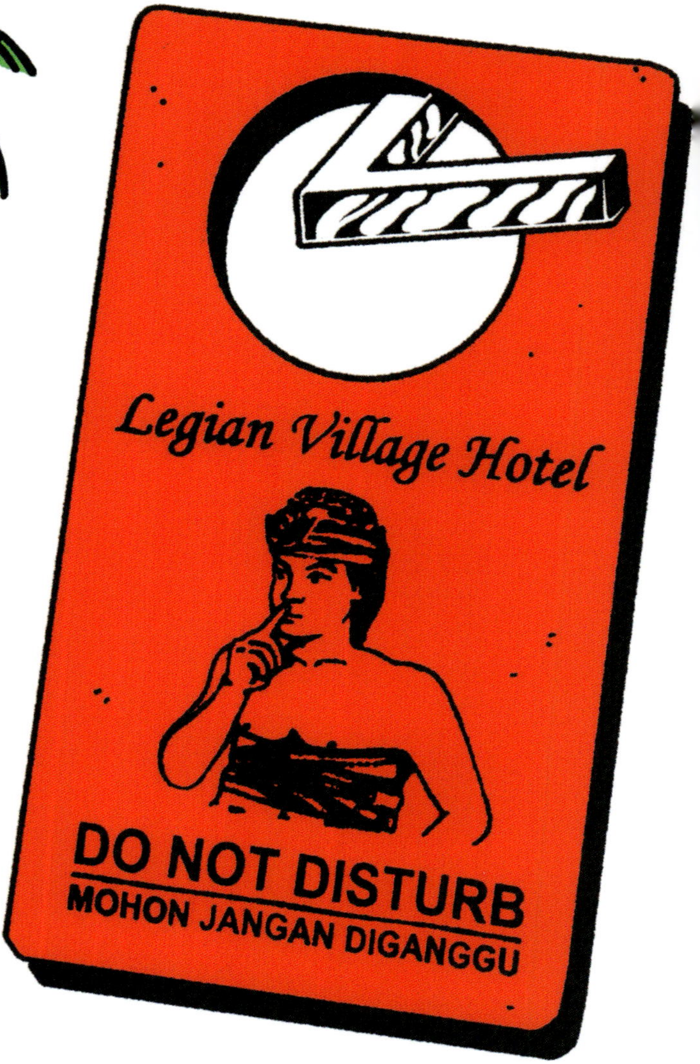

Legian Village Hotel

DO NOT DISTURB

MOHON JANGAN DIGANGGU

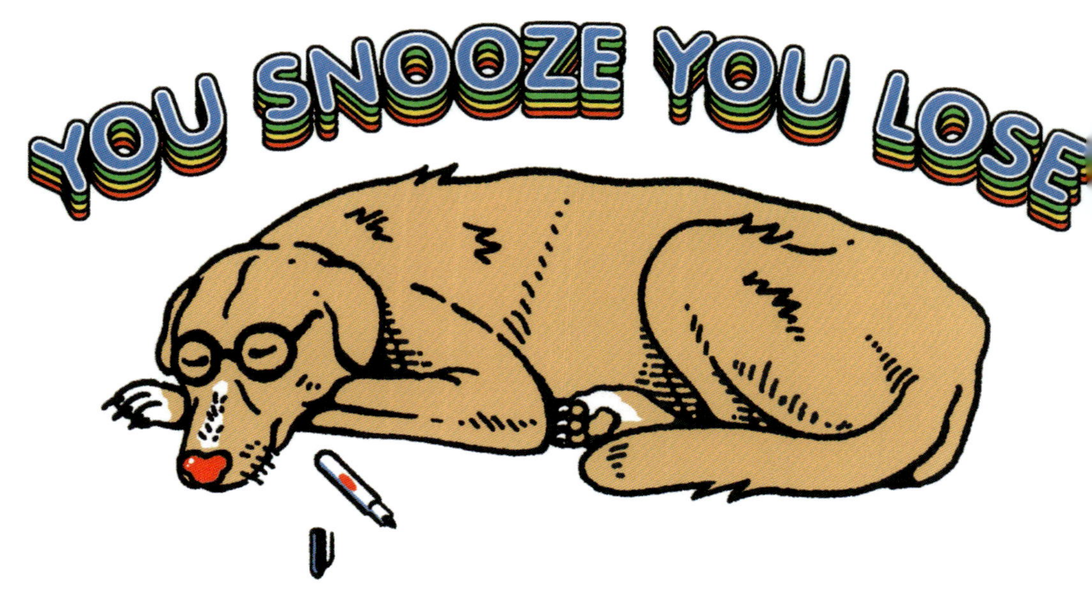

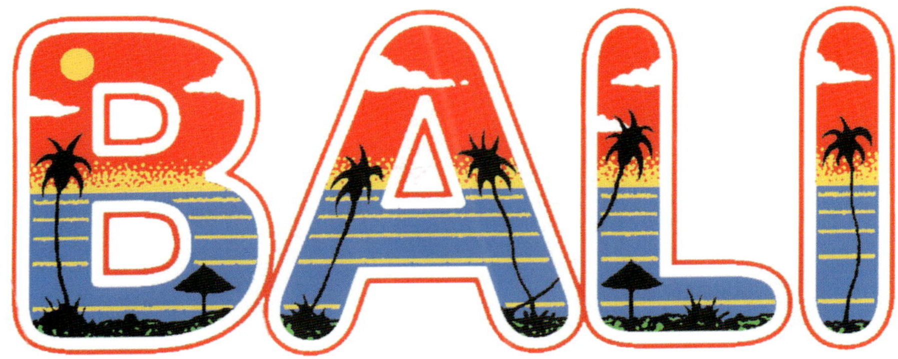
BALI

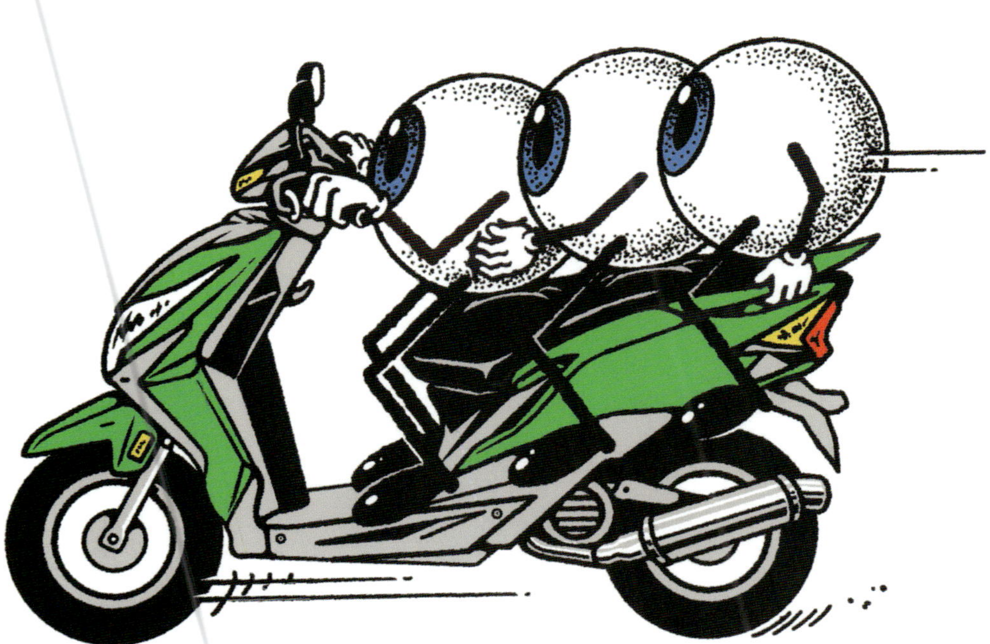

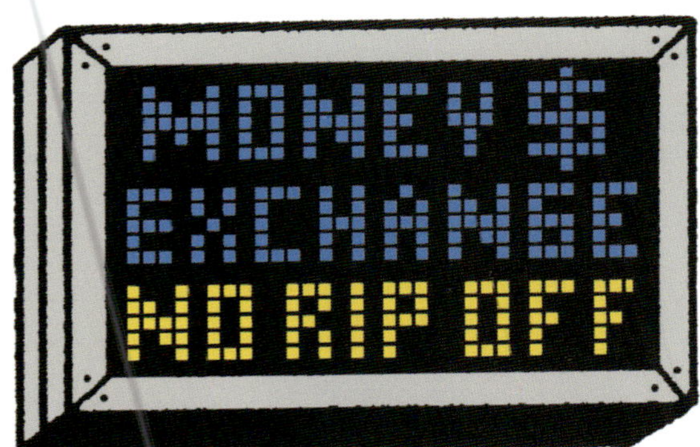
MONEY$
EXCHANGE
NO RIP OFF

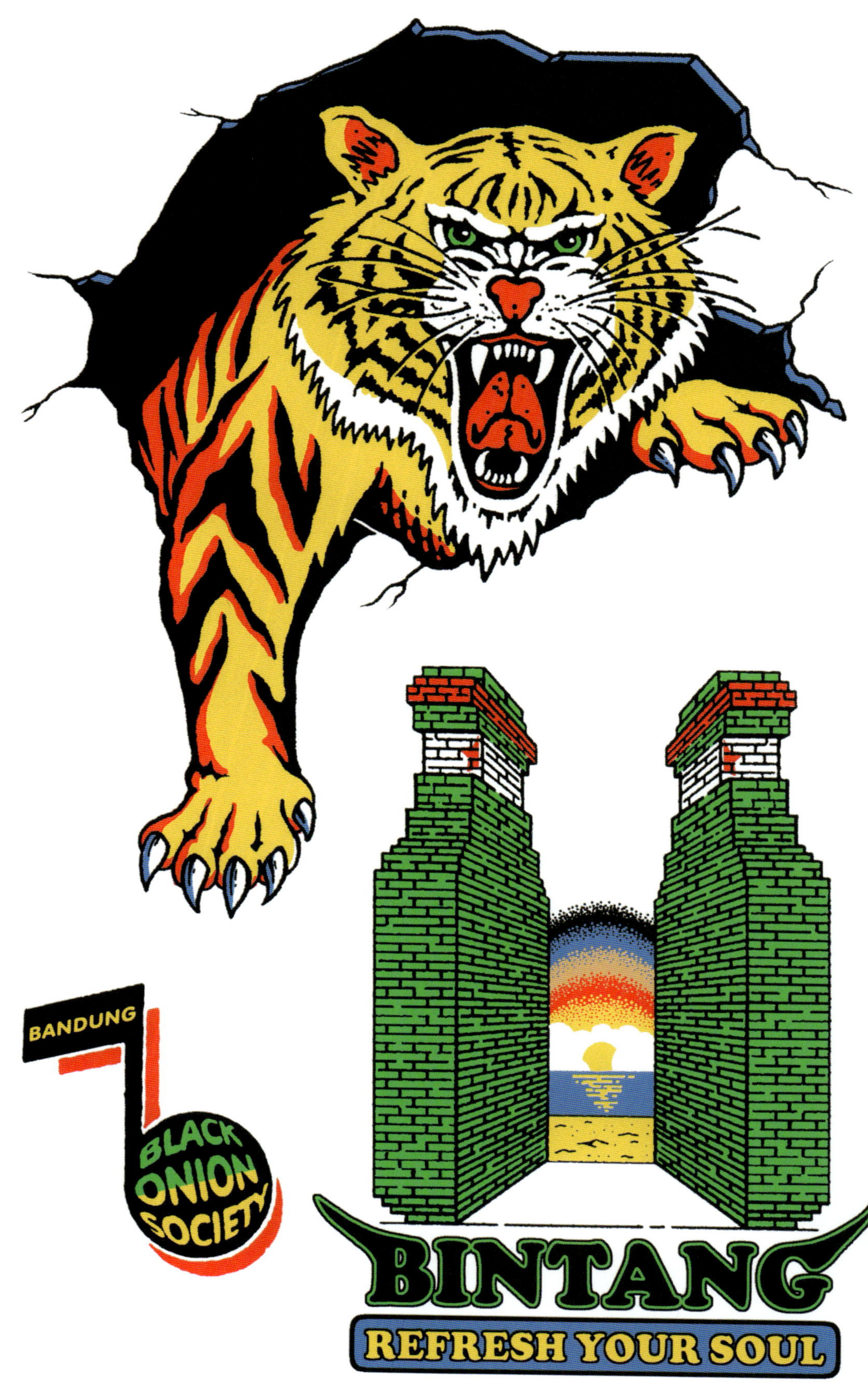
BANDUNG
BLACK
ONION
SOCIETY
BINTANG
REFRESH YOUR SOUL

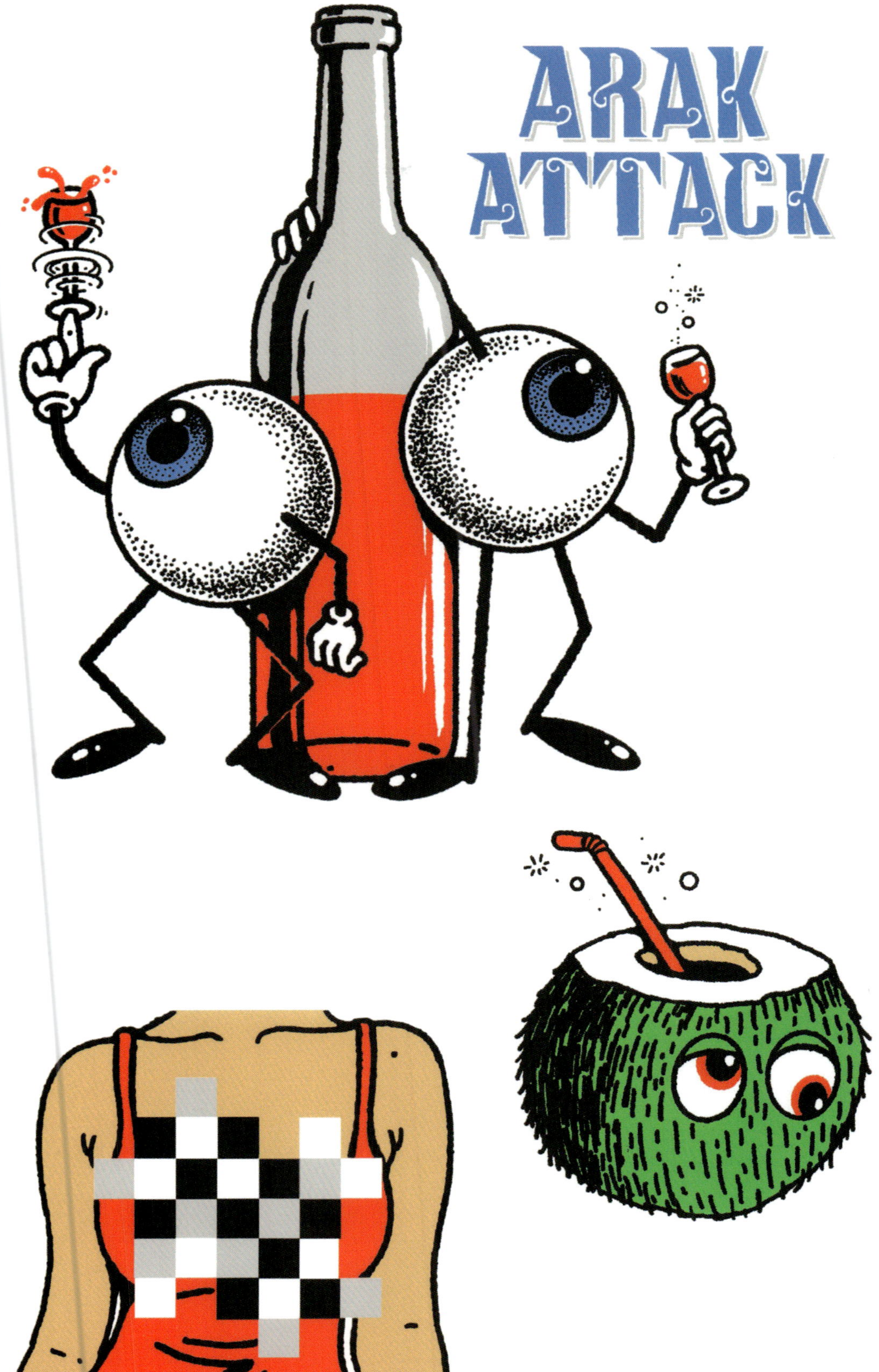
ARAK
ATTACK

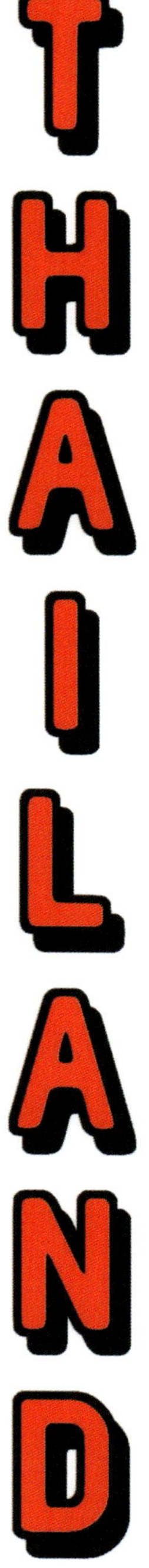
THAILAND

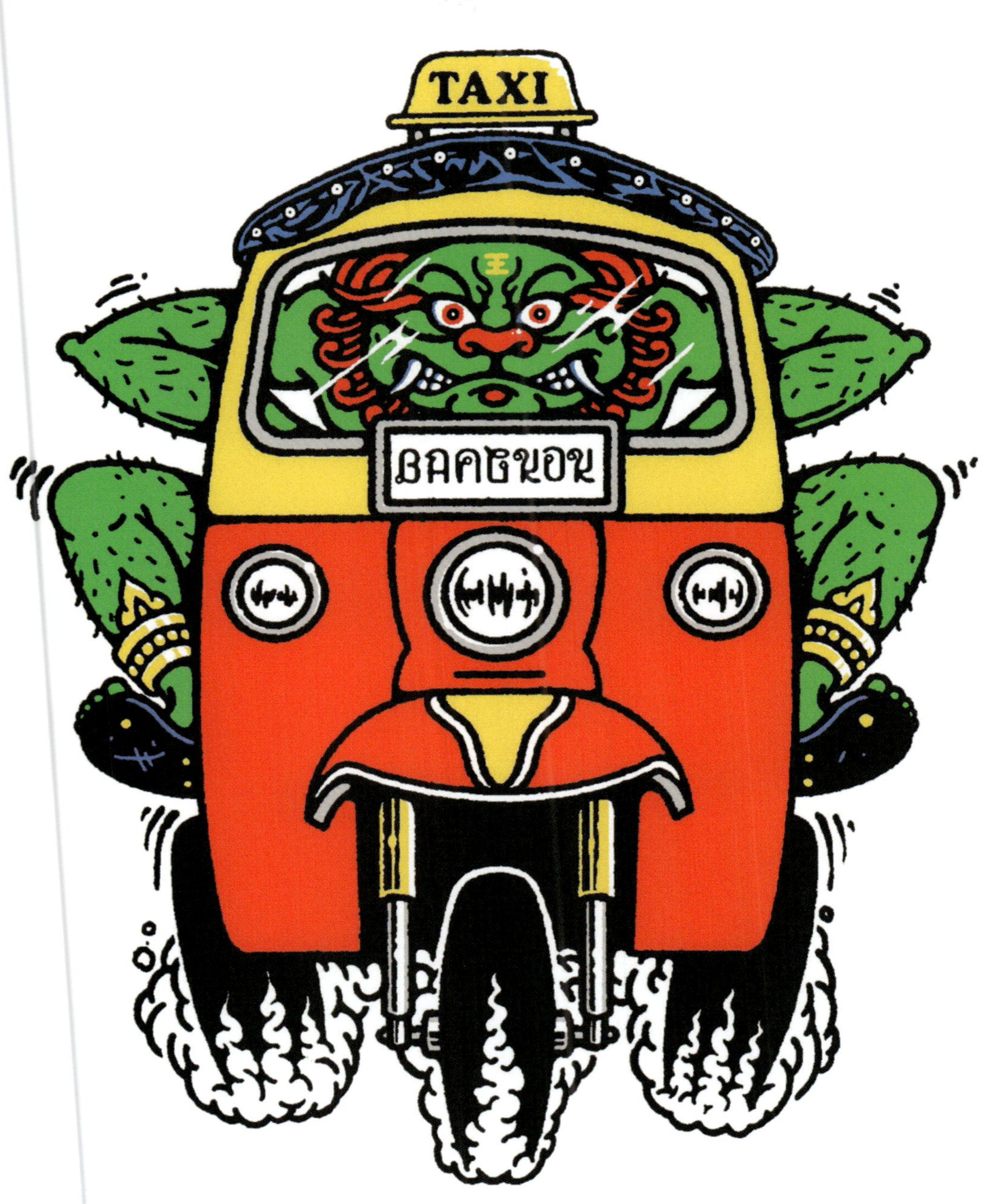
TAXI
BANGKOK

THAILAND

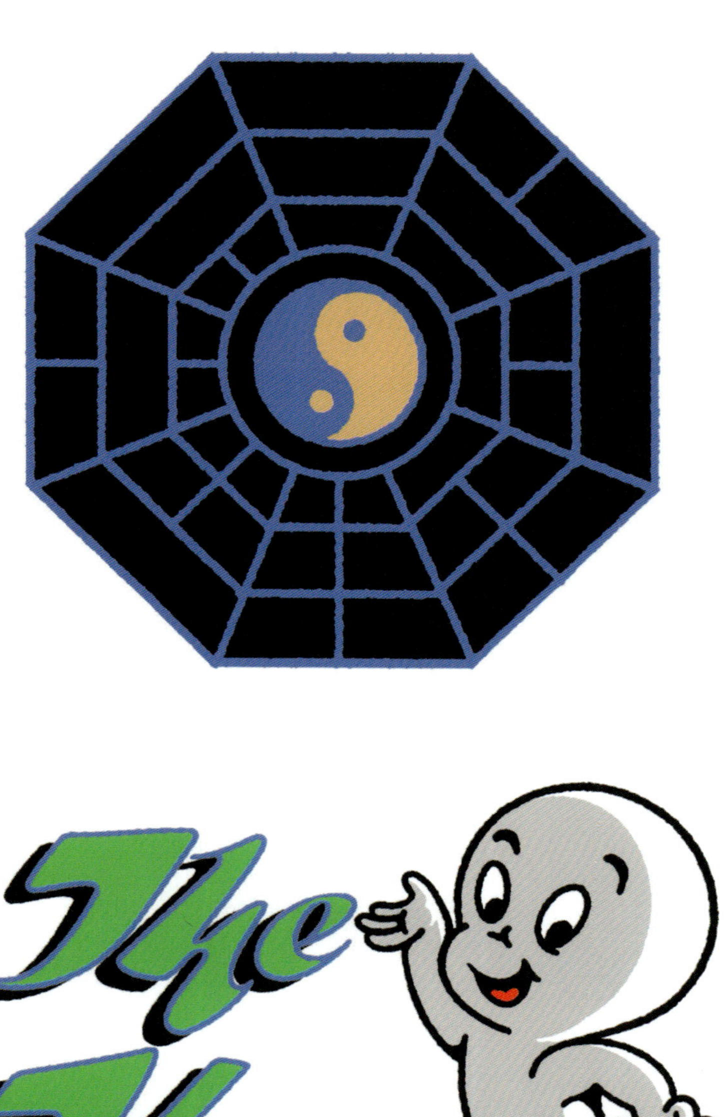

The Floor Seasons

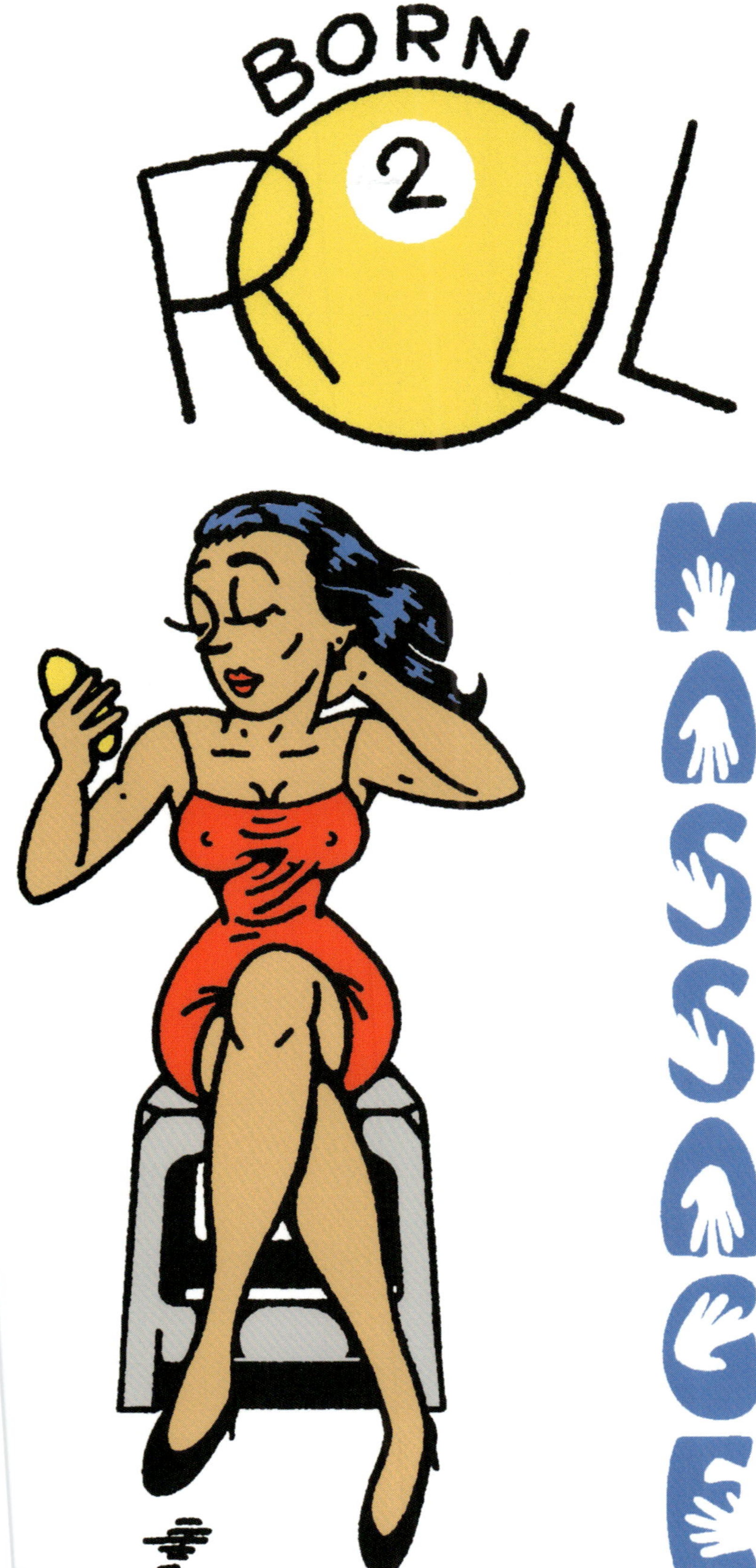
BORN
2
ROLL
MASSAGE

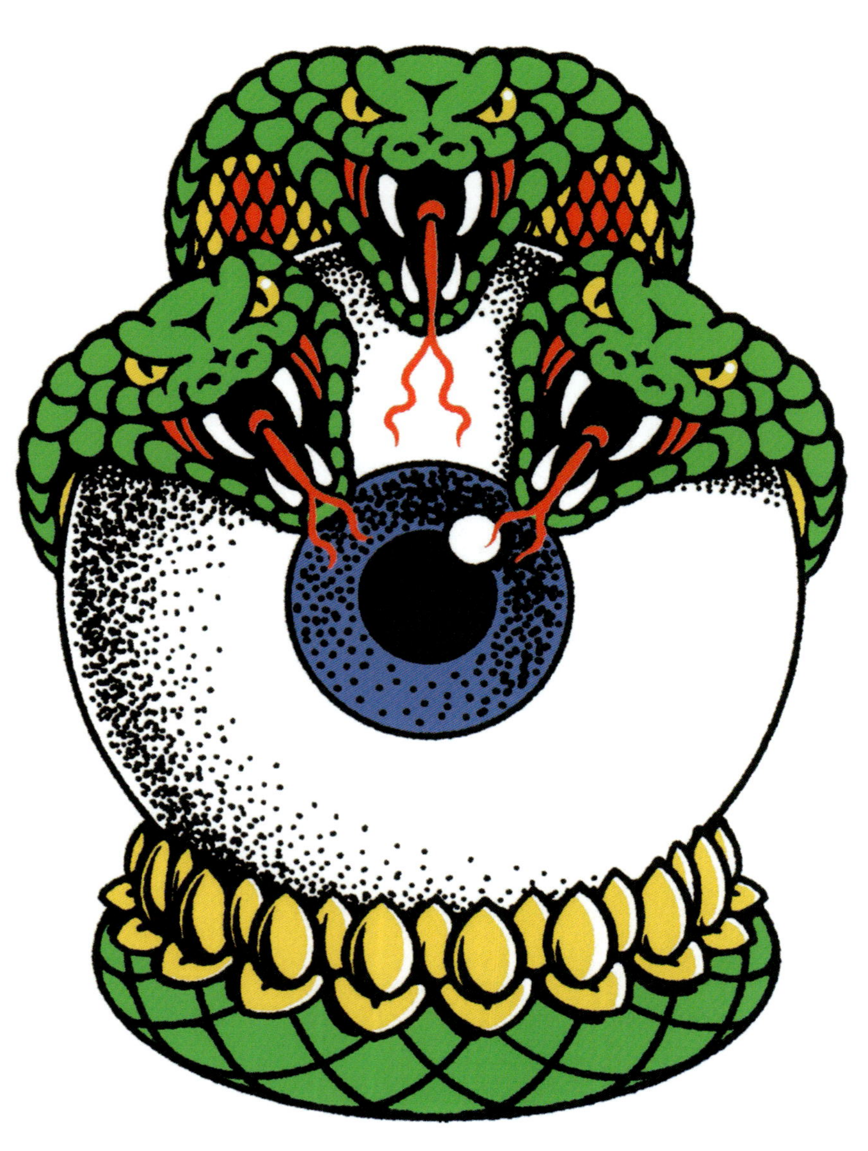

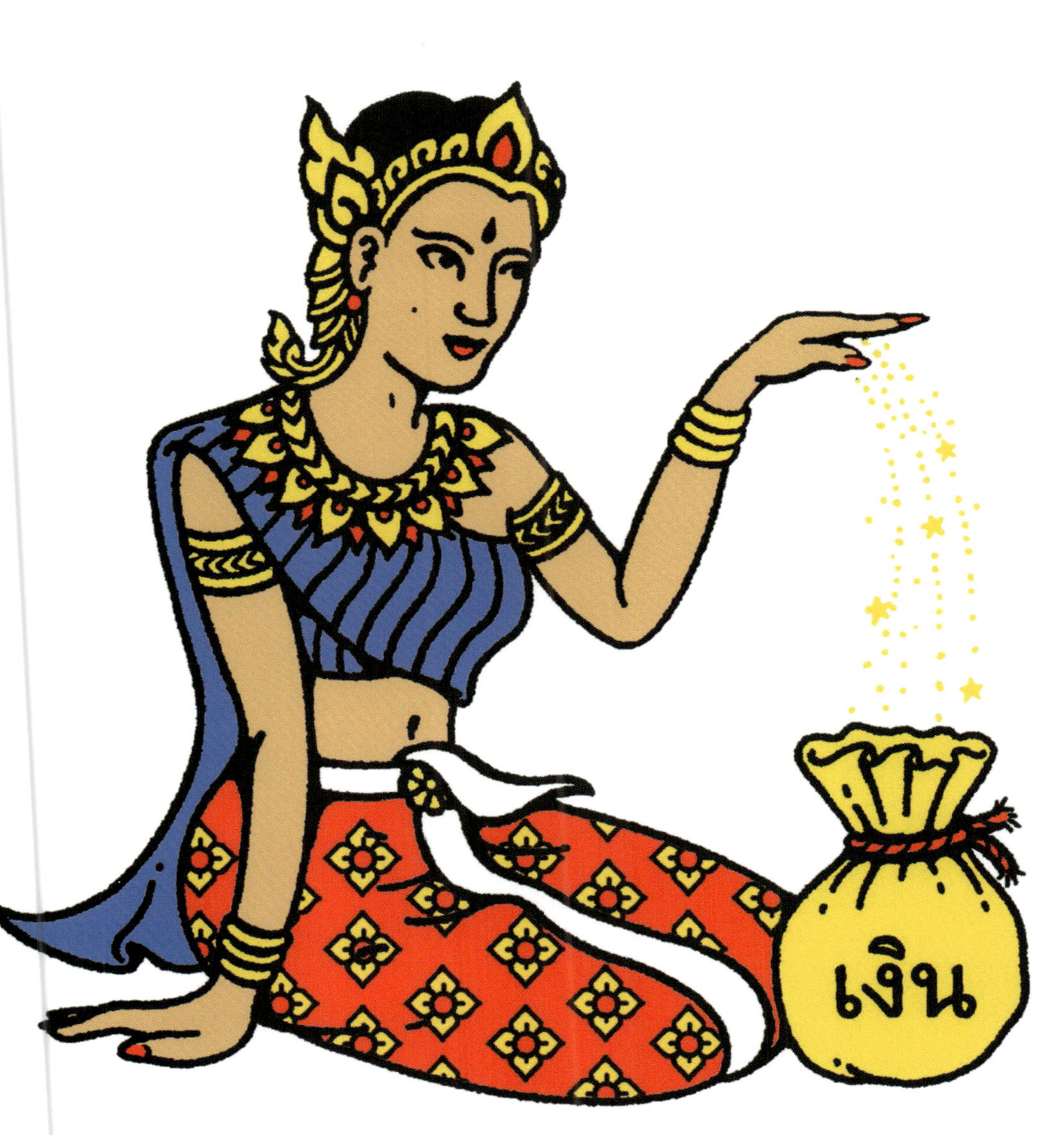
เงิน

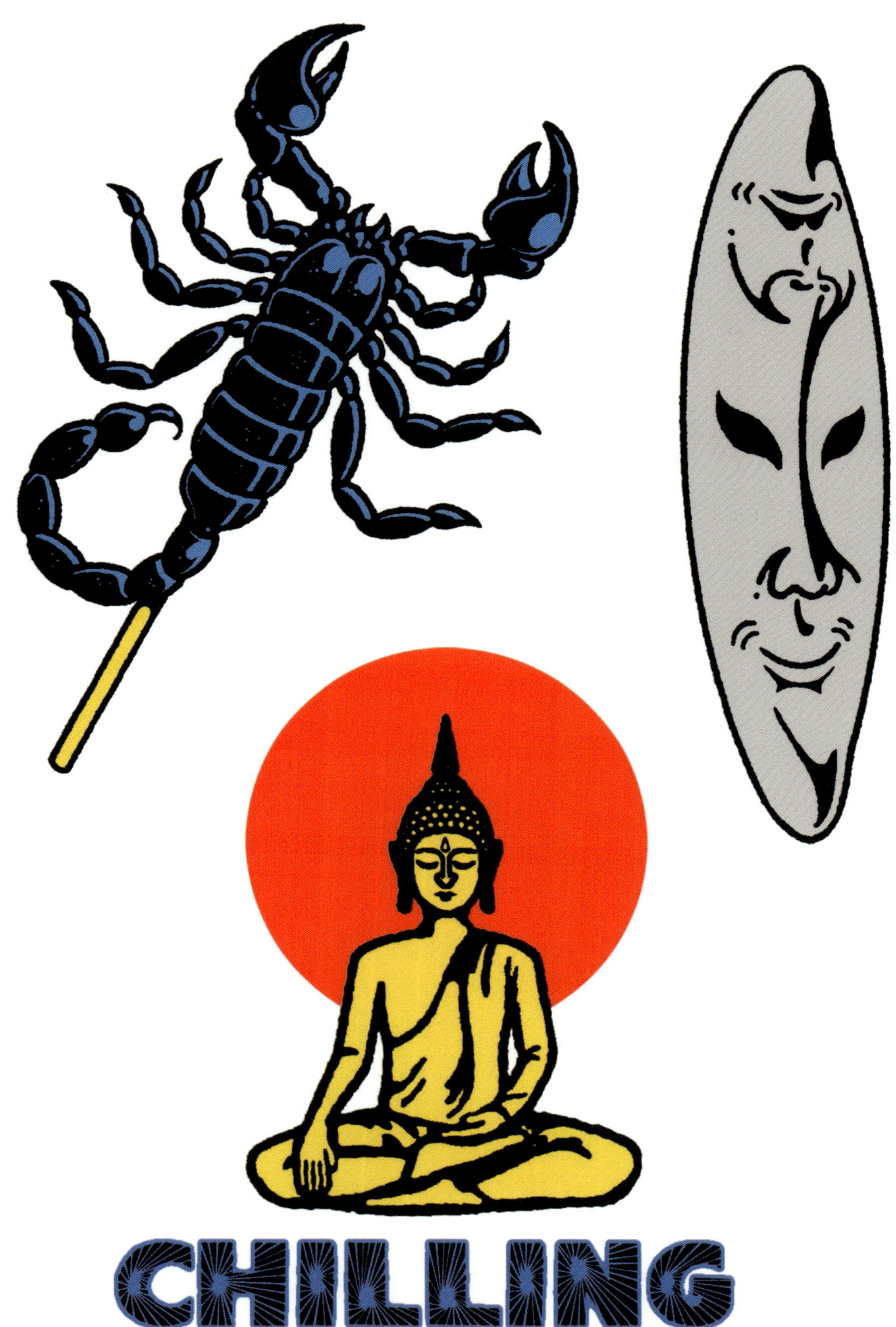
CHILLING
& HEALING

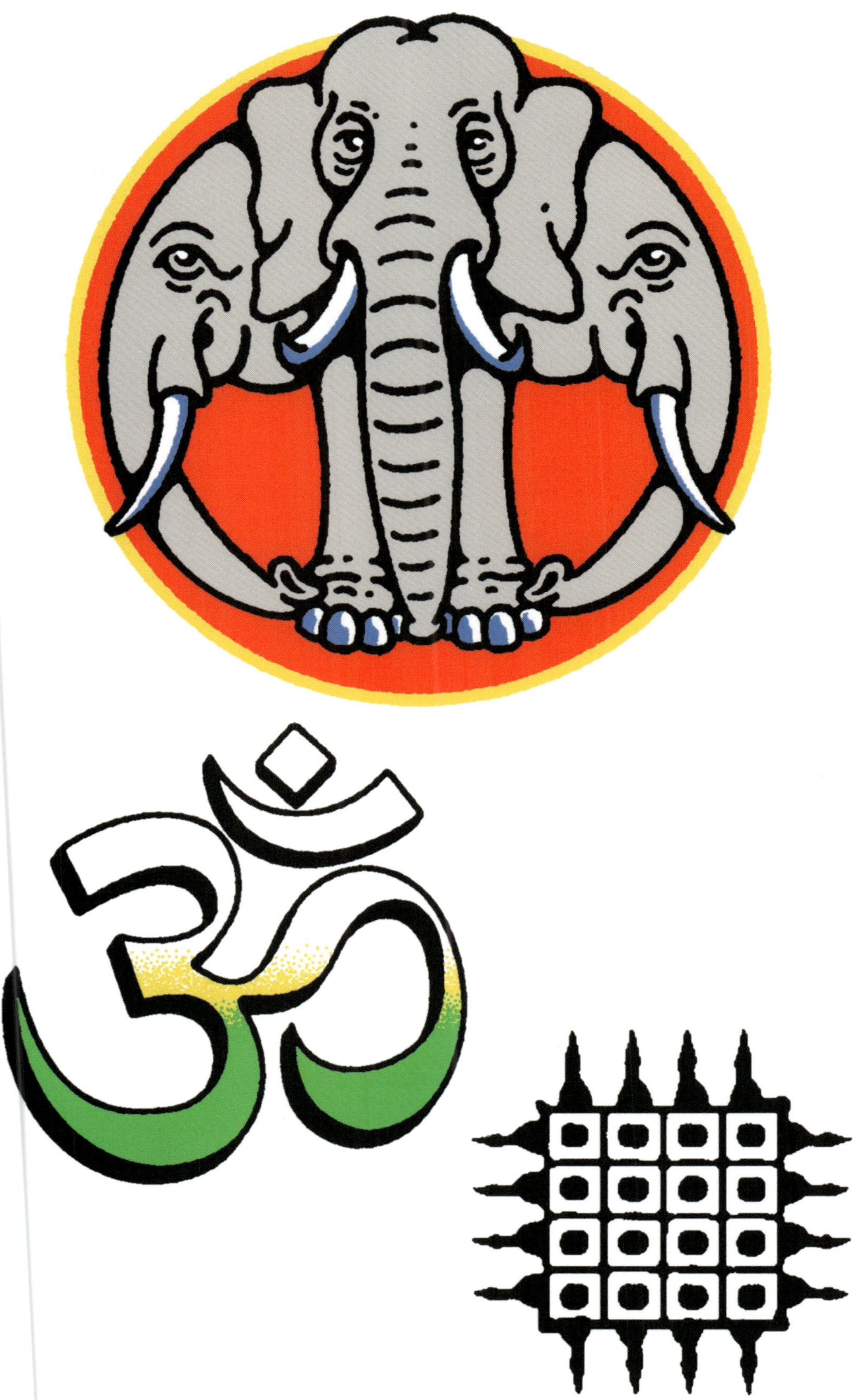

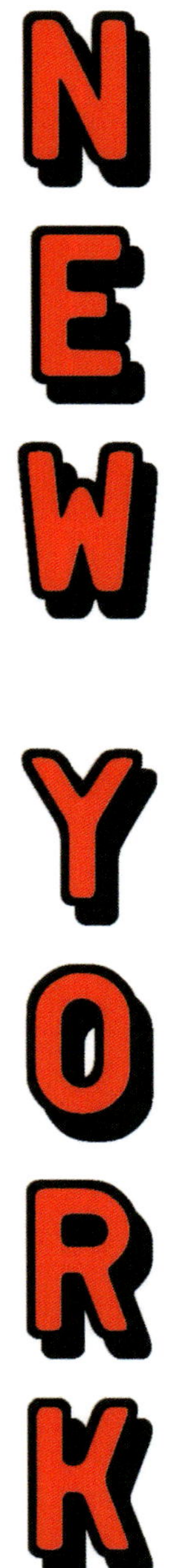
NEW YORK

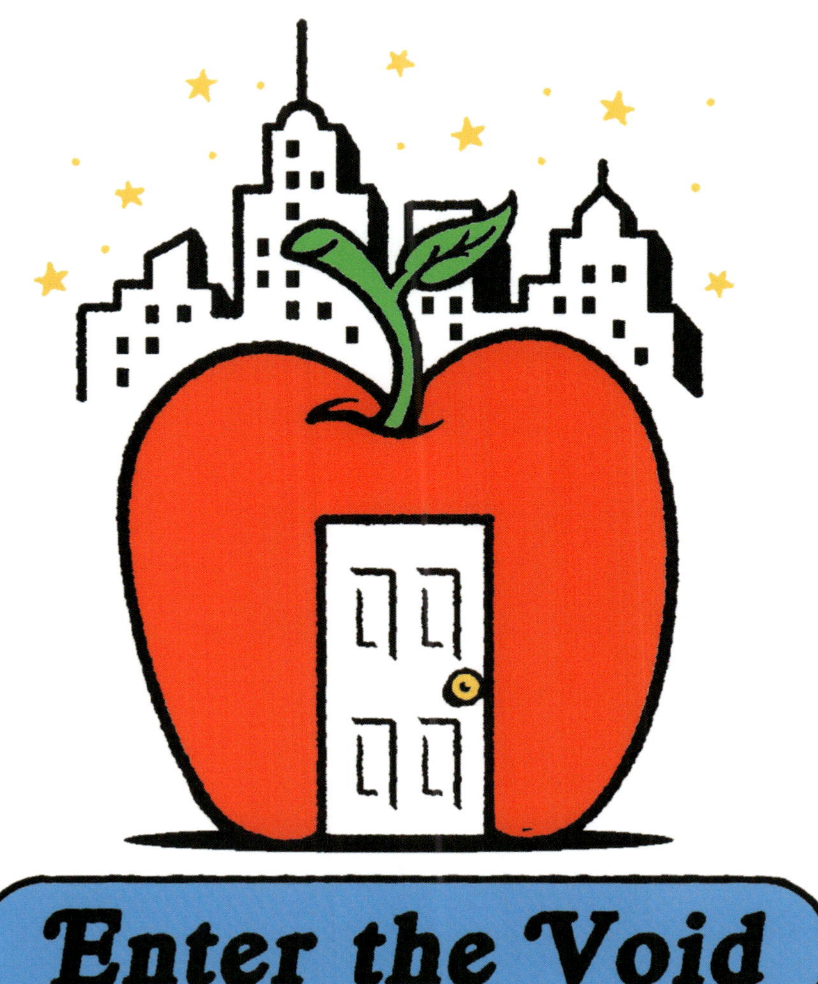
Enter the Void

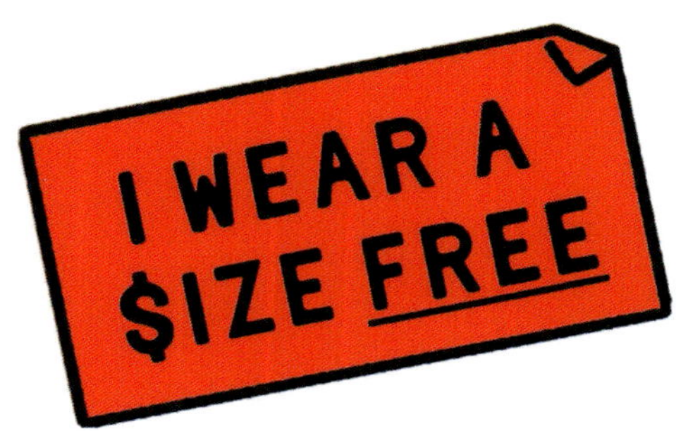

I SU AMOR DE TU VISA NY

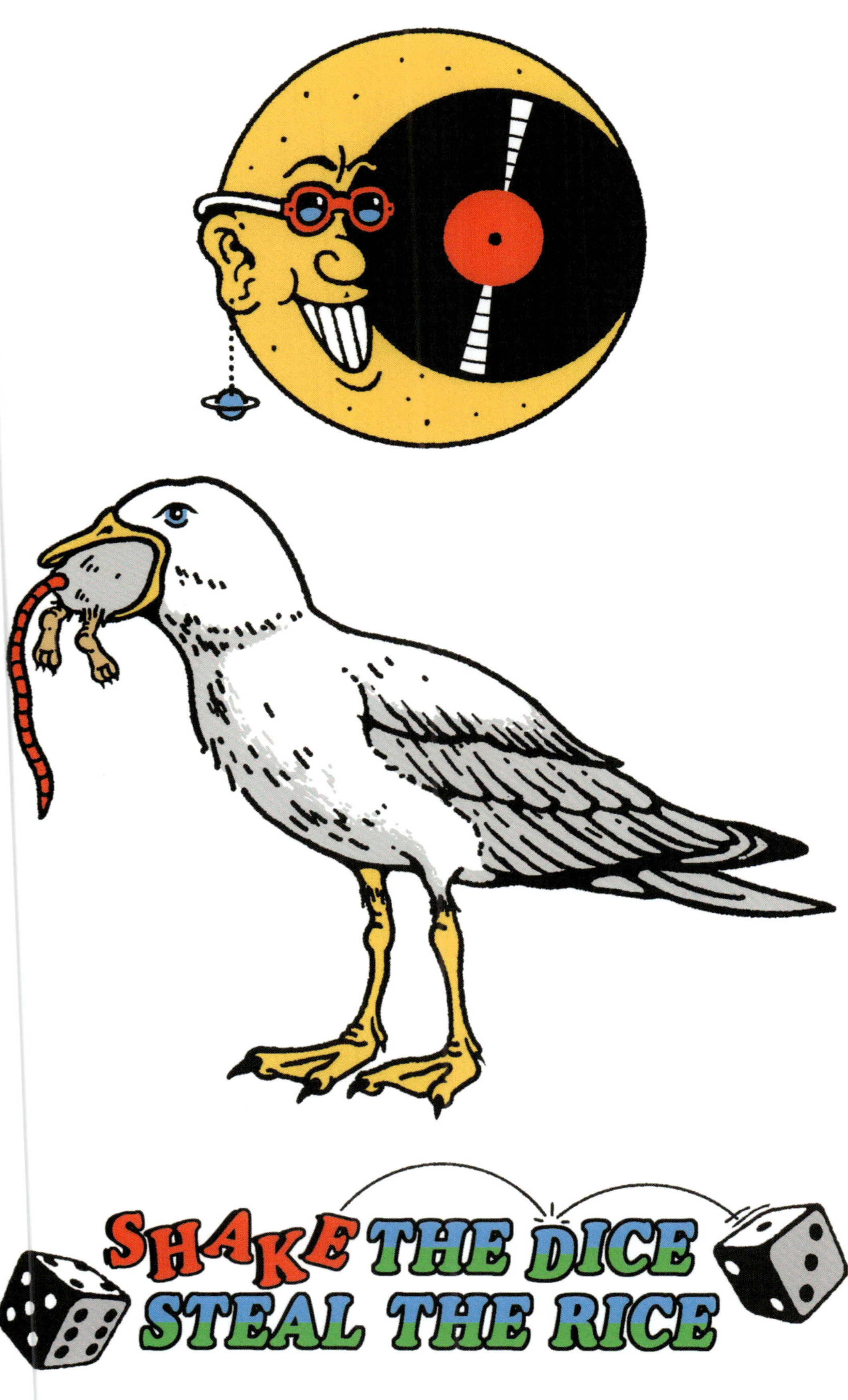
SHAKE THE DICE
STEAL THE RICE

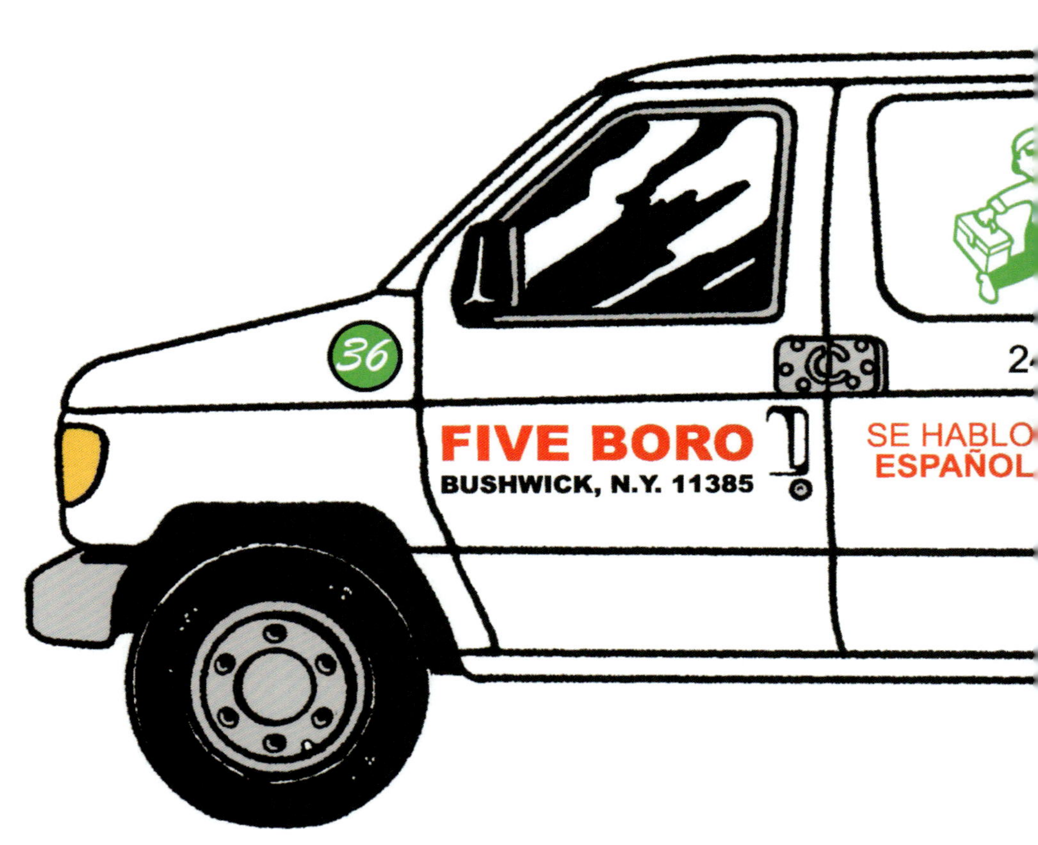
36
FIVE BORO
BUSHWICK, N.Y. 11385
SE HABLO
ESPAÑOL

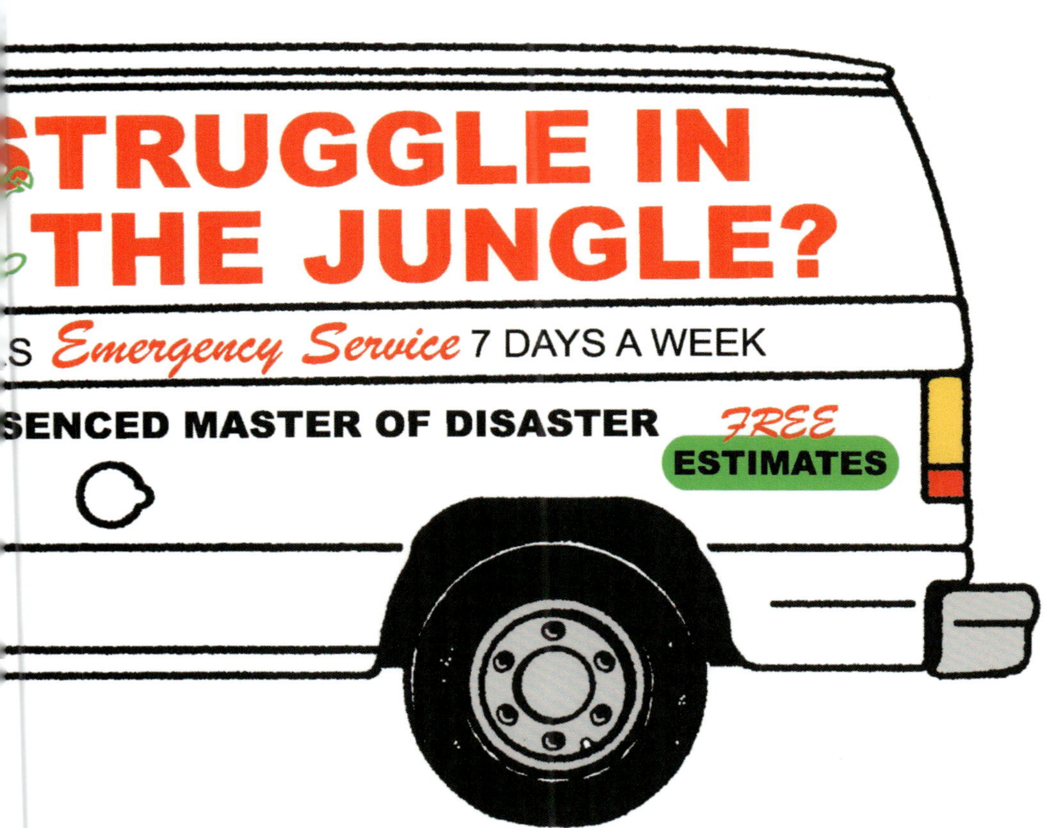
STRUGGLE IN
THE JUNGLE?
S Emergency Service 7 DAYS A WEEK
SENCED MASTER OF DISASTER
FREE
ESTIMATES

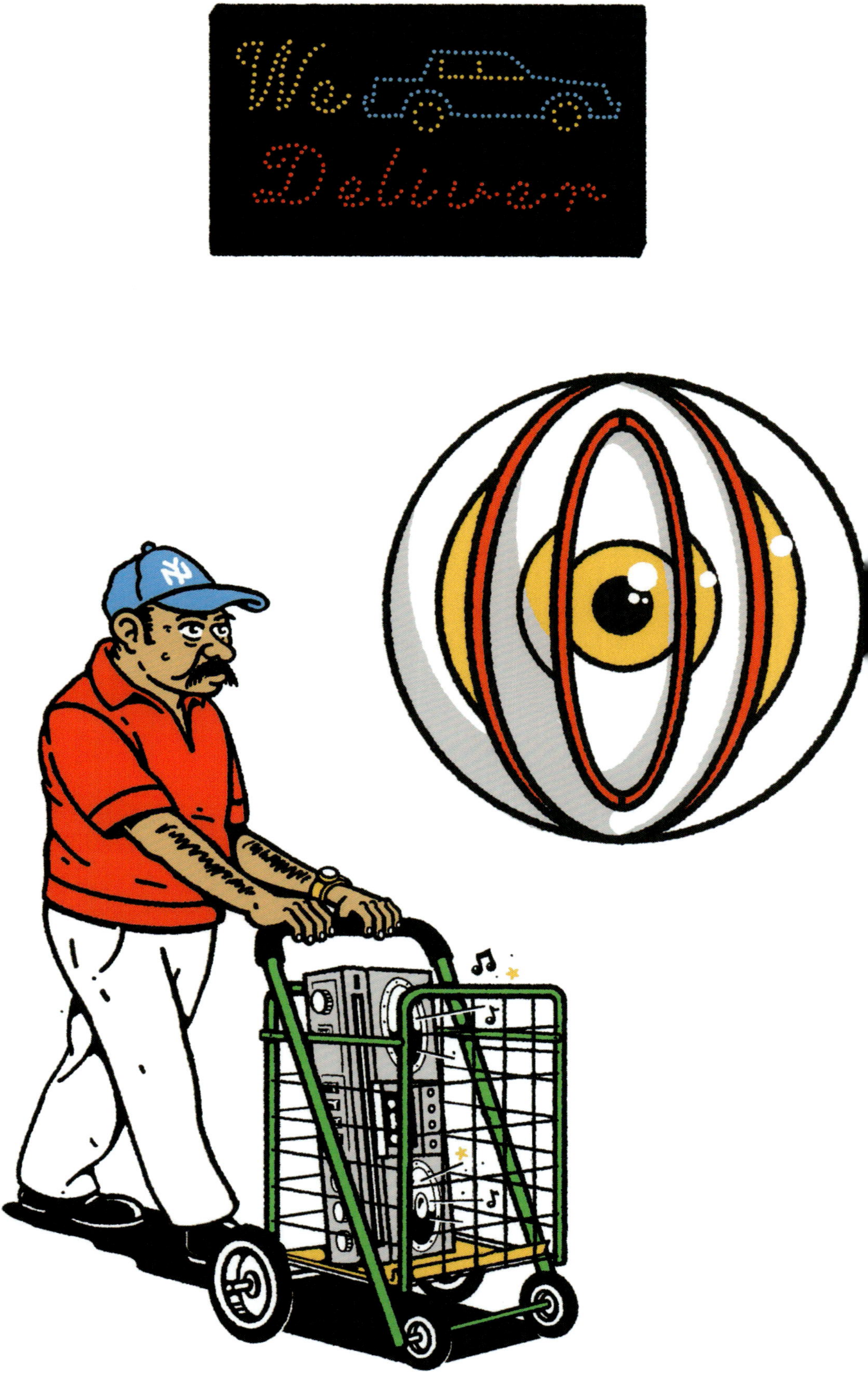

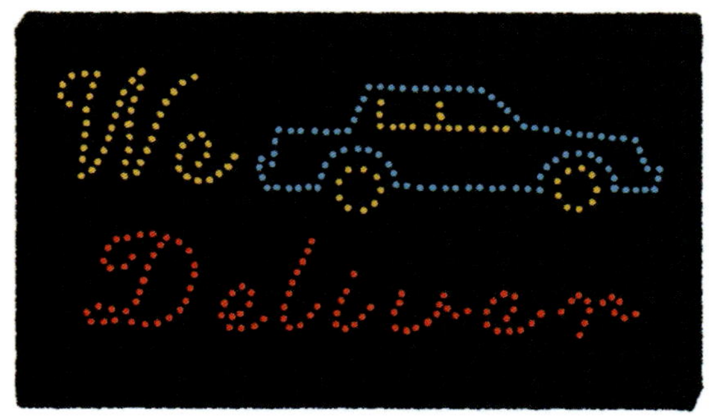
We
Deliver

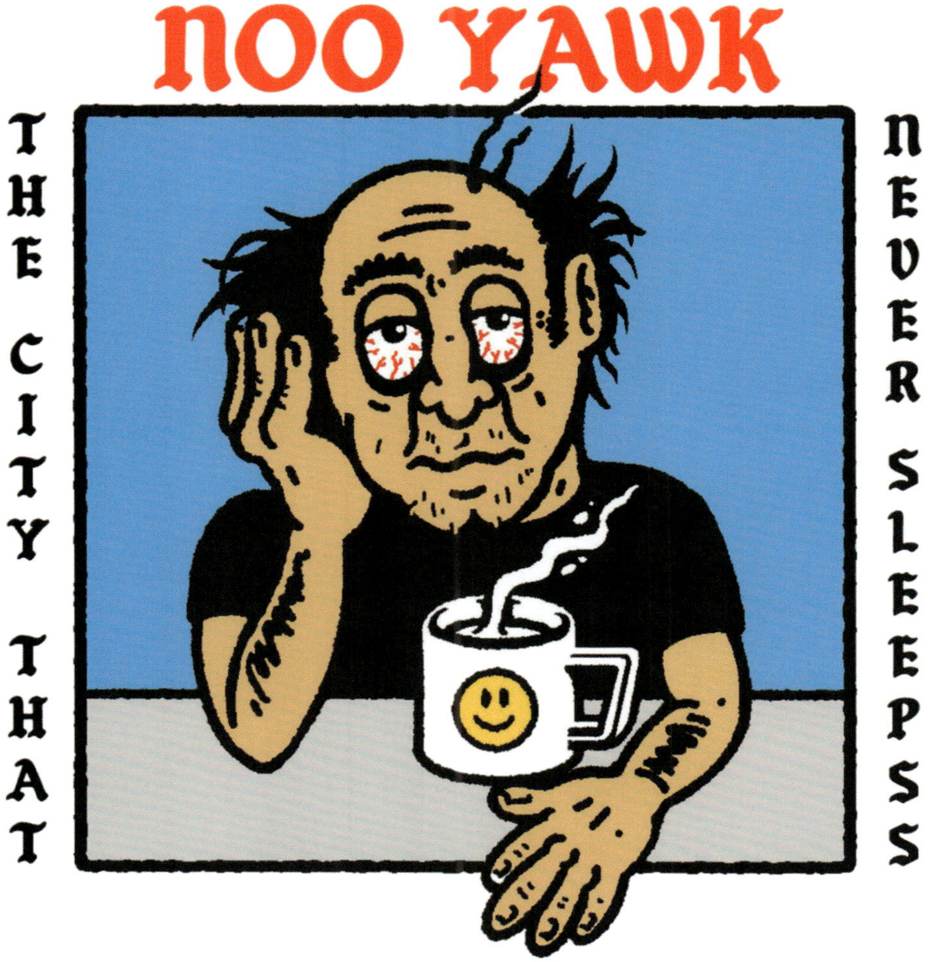

NOO YAWK

THE CITY THAT

NEVER SLEEPSS

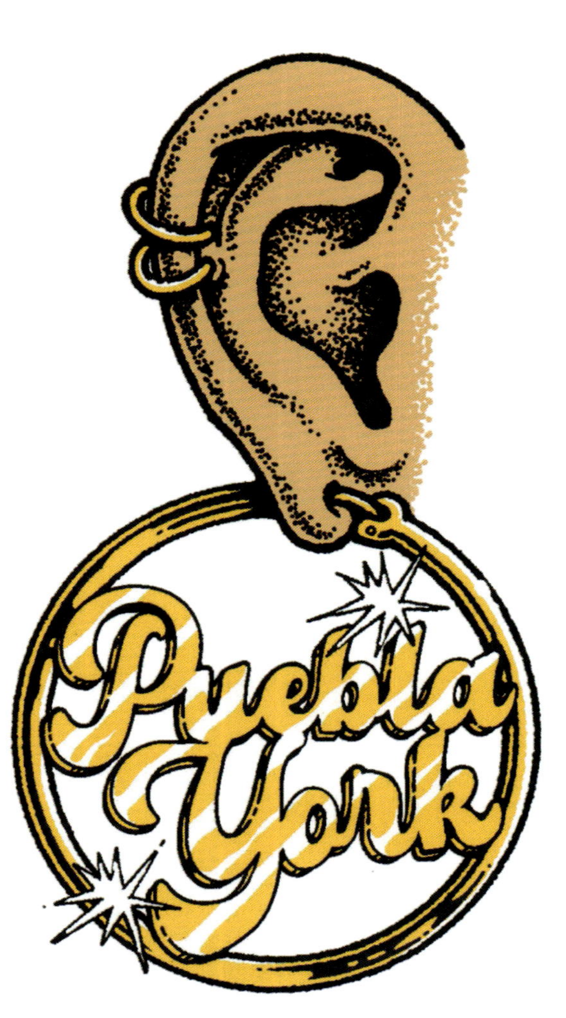
Puebla
York

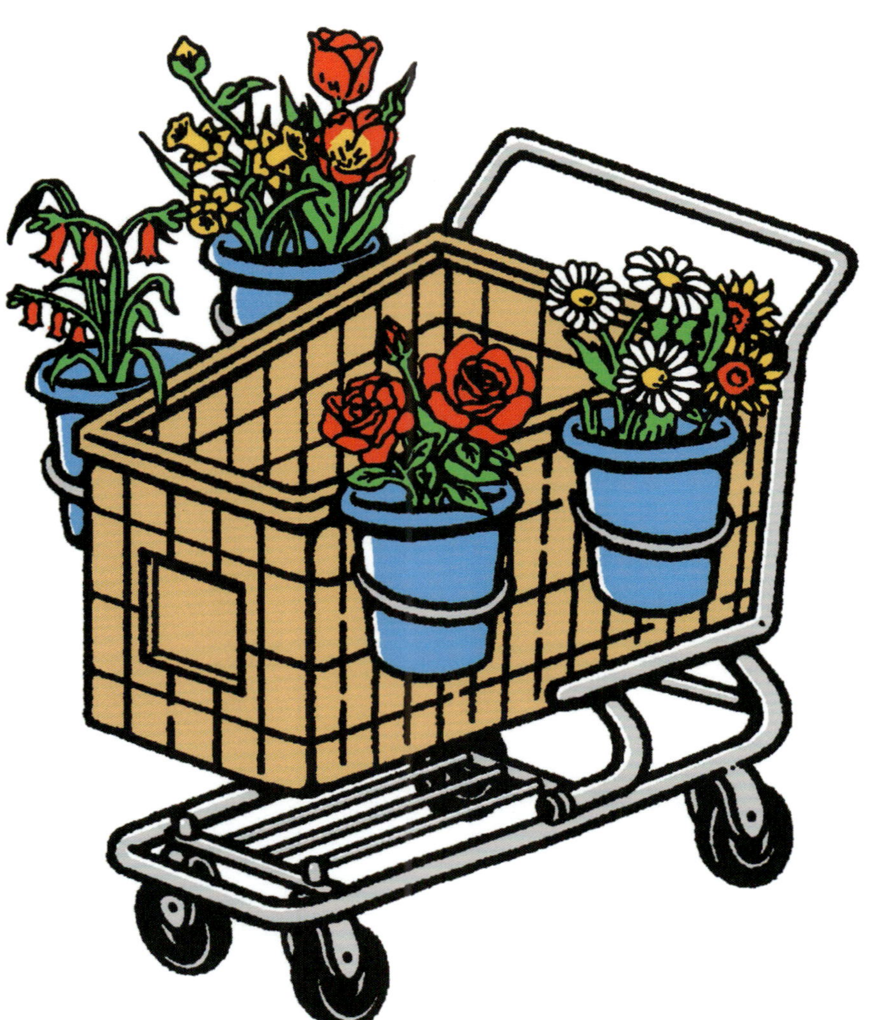

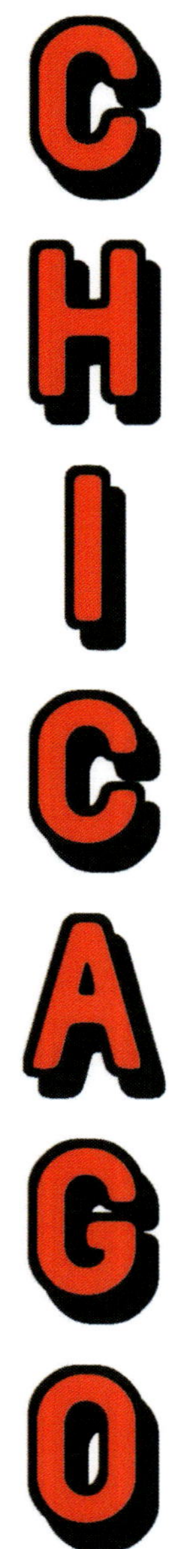
CHICAGO

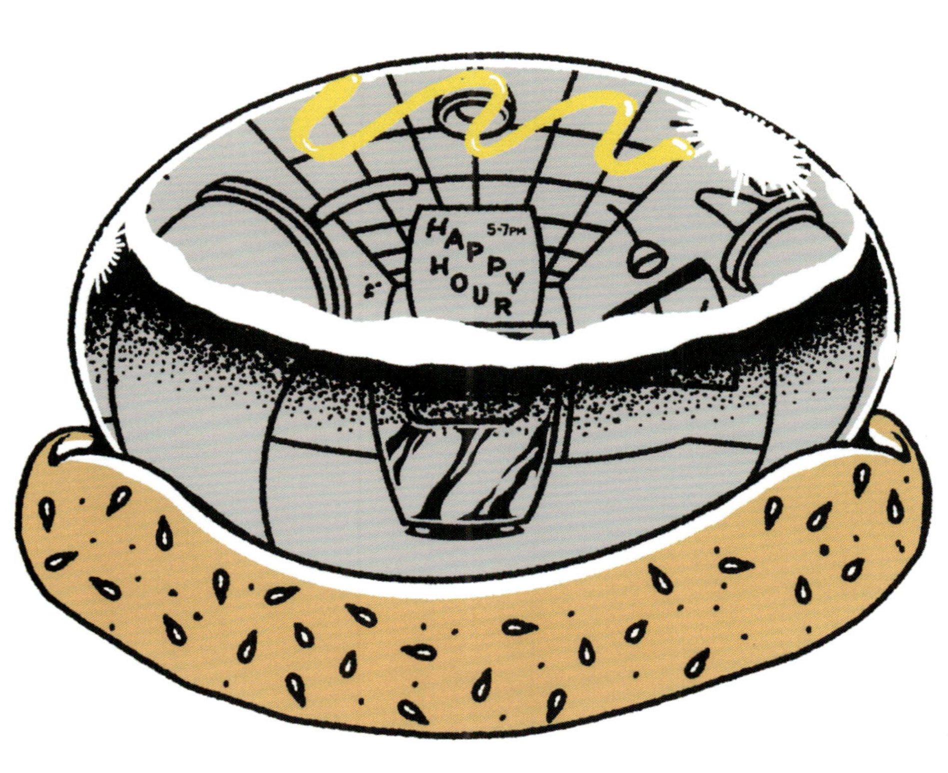
HAPPY HOUR
5-7PM

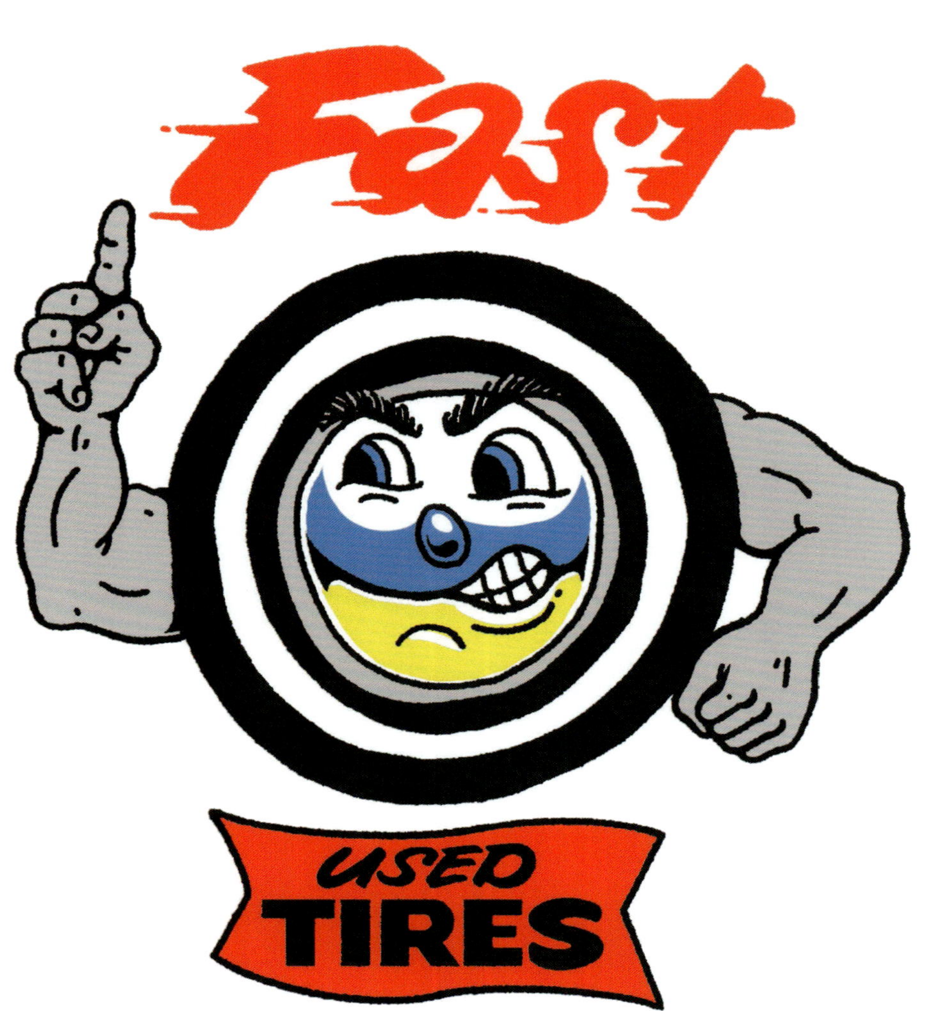
Fast
USED
TIRES

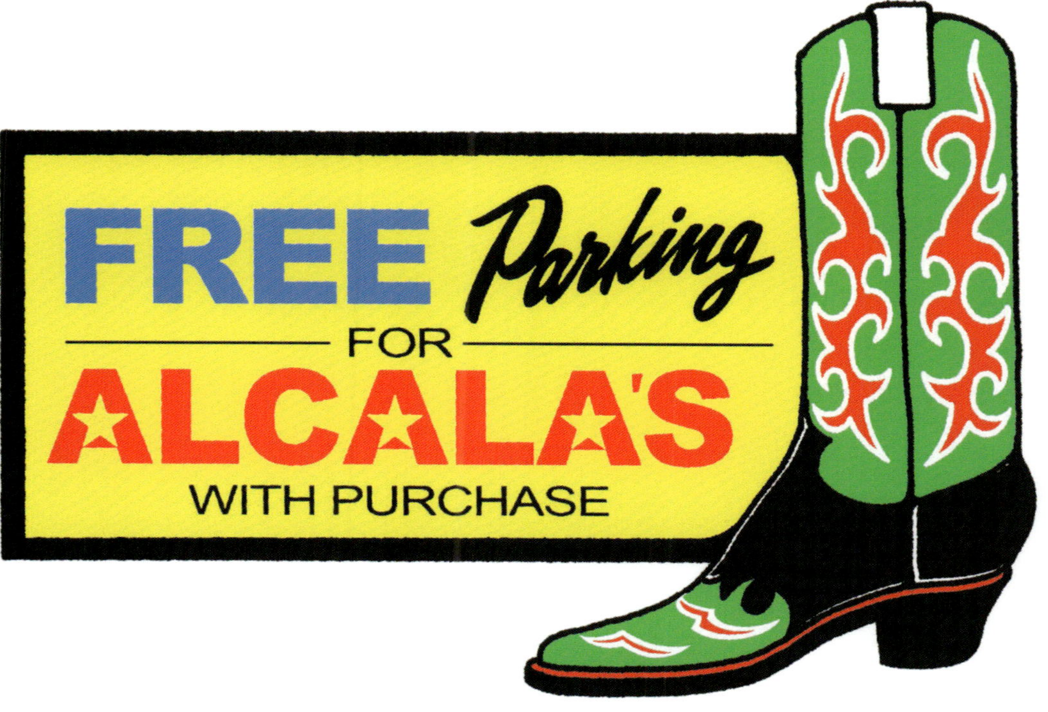
FREE Parking
FOR
ALCALA'S
WITH PURCHASE

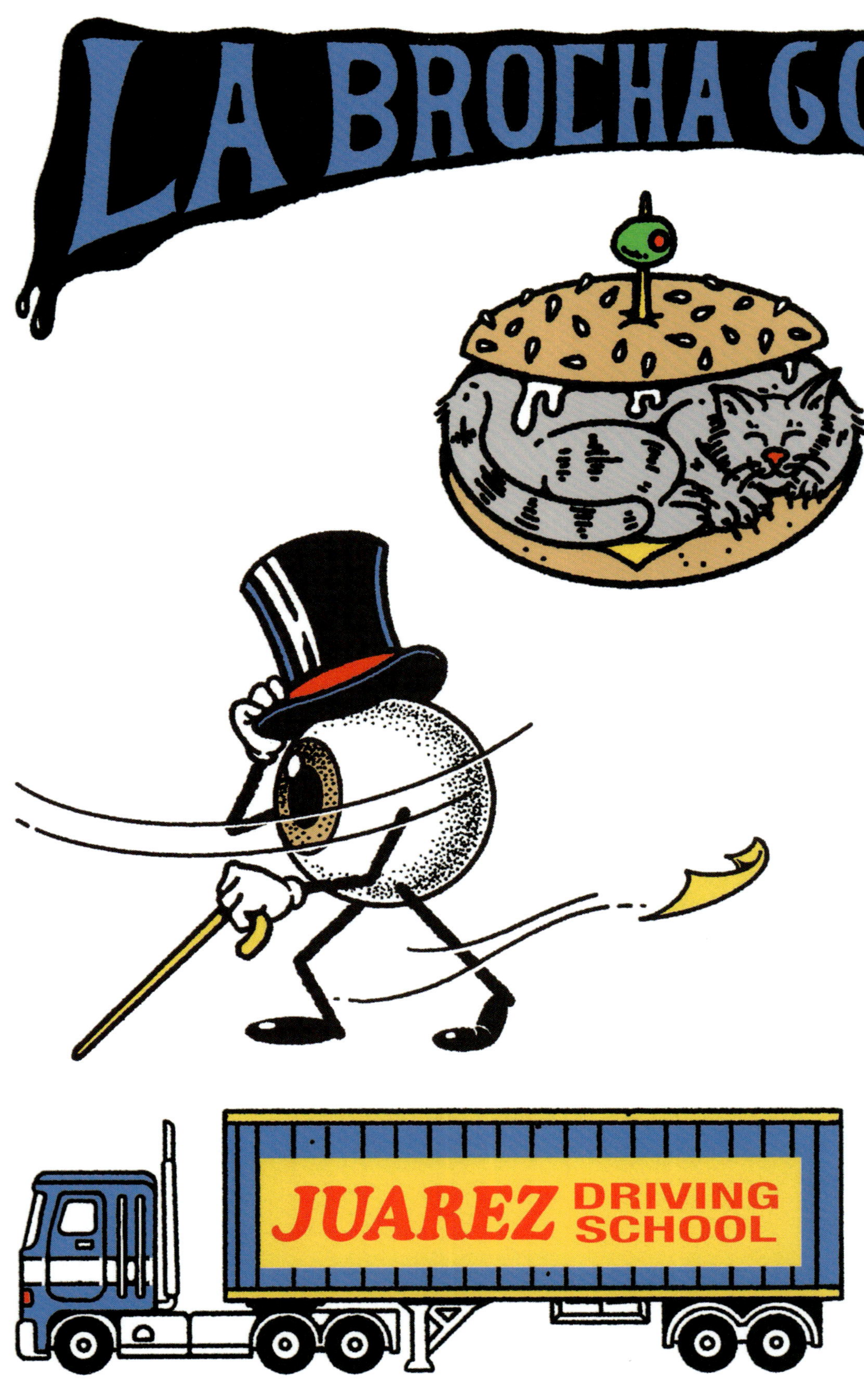
LA BROCHA GO
JUAREZ DRIVING SCHOOL

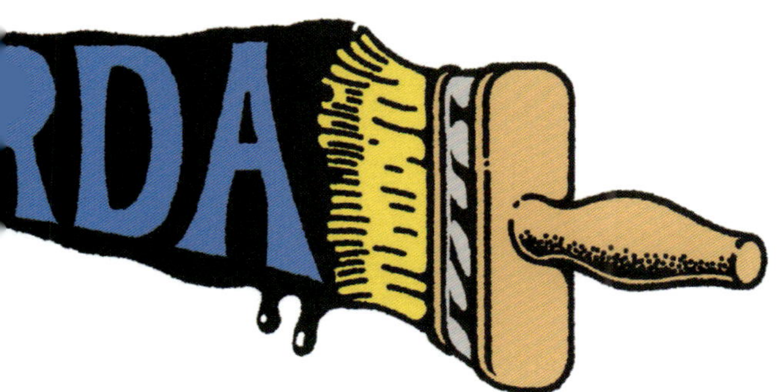

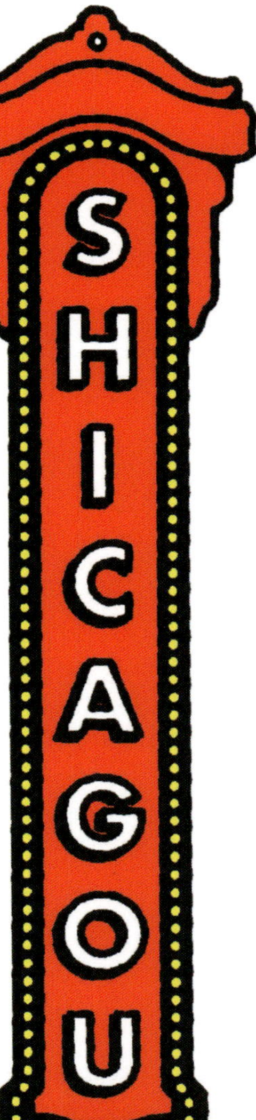

PILSEN

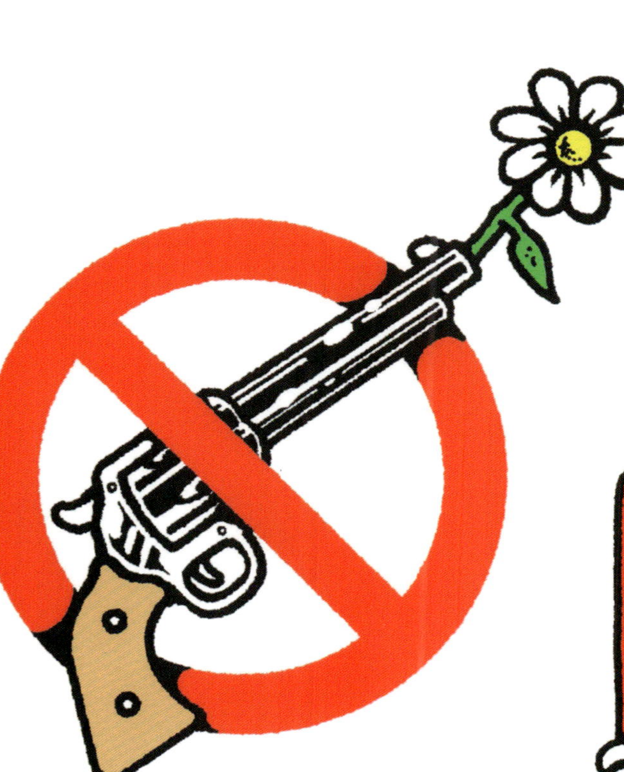

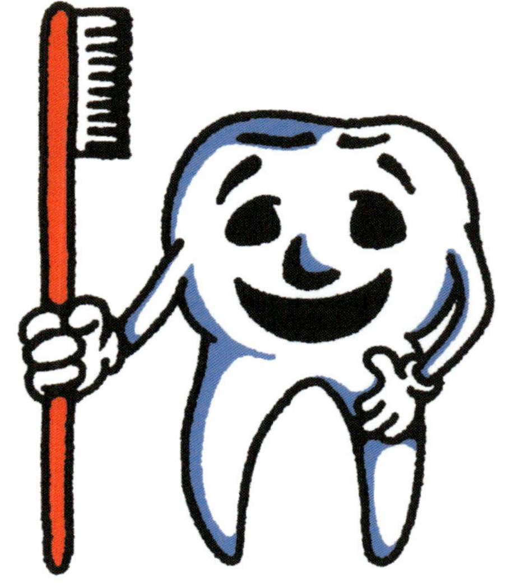

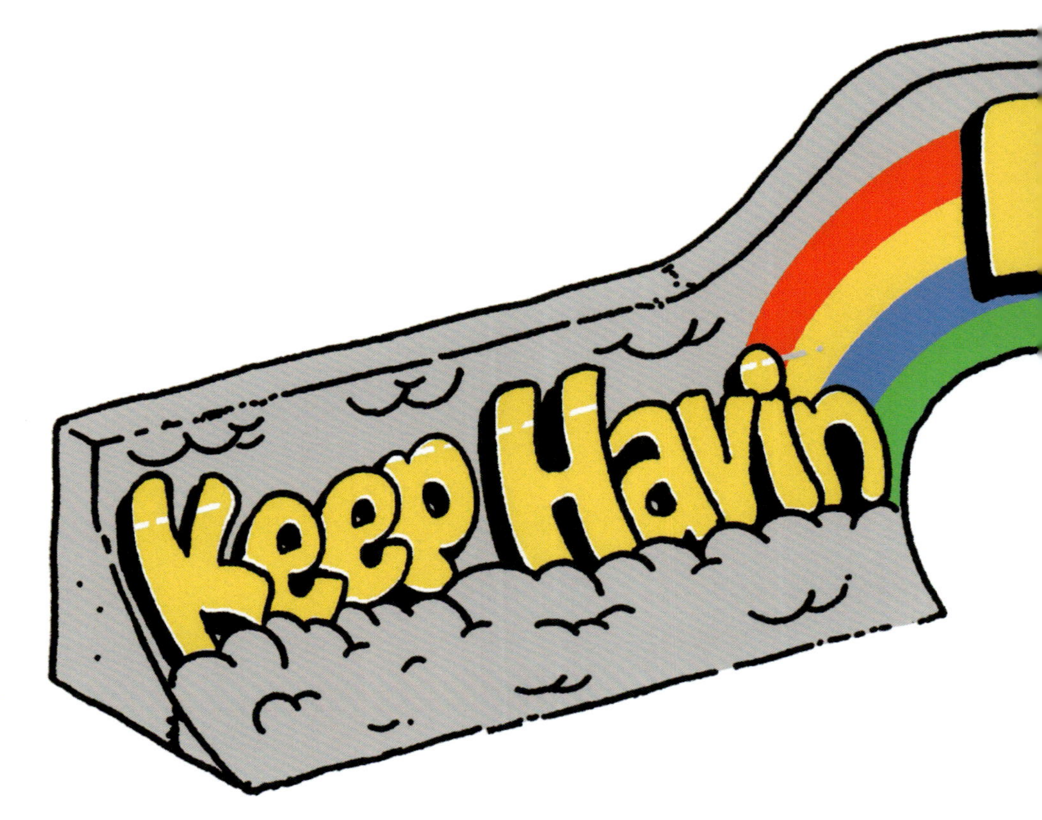
Keep Havin

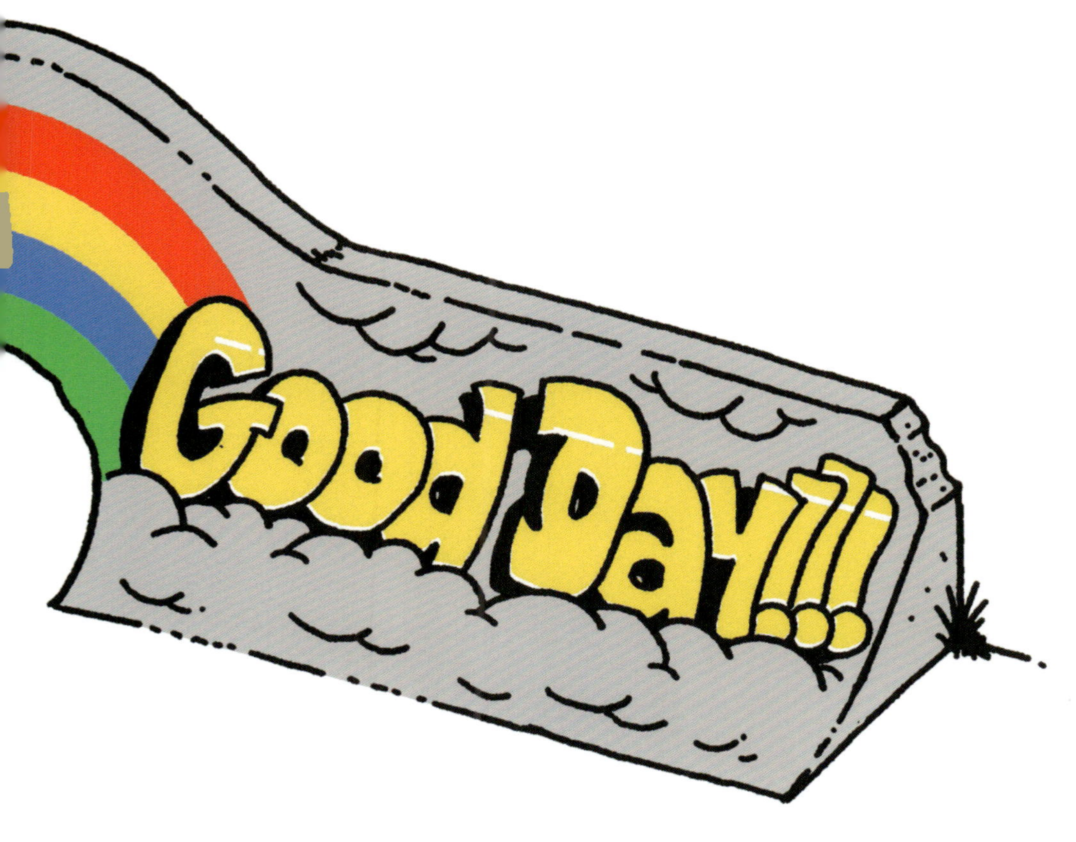
Good Day!!!

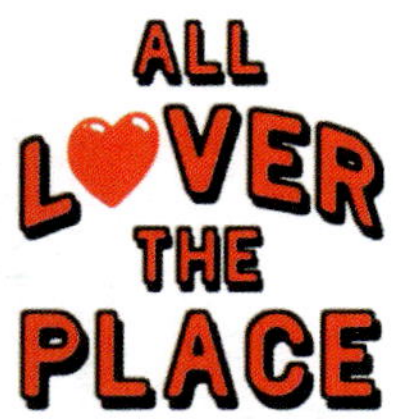

Illustration & Layout
Daniel Shepard
Daniel-Shepard.com

Published by Blurring Books
Number 20 in the LSP Series
Blurringbooks.com

1st Edition, 2025
300 copies
Printed in the U.K.
ISBN: 978-1-963814-24-8